Preface

Welcome to the exciting world of TAP AND LEARN For Class 5! This book, designed for students, is an engaging and comprehensive introduction to computer science. Our goal is to spark curiosity and provide a strong foundation in computer literacy, preparing young minds for a future where technology plays a central role. In today's world, computers are everywhere. From schools and homes to offices and shops, they have become an integral part of our lives. Understanding how computers work and how to use them effectively is crucial for success in almost every field. This book aims to make learning about computers fun and easy for young students.

This book is structured to introduce students gradually to the world of computers, ensuring that they understand each concept thoroughly before moving on to the next. Here's a brief overview of what you will find in the chapters: We begin with the basics, answering the fundamental question: What is a computer? Students will learn about the various types of computers and their uses in different environments. This chapter introduces the physical parts of a computer. Students will learn about input devices like the keyboard and mouse, output devices like monitors and printers, and the central processing unit (CPU) which acts as the brain of the computer. Here, we explain the difference between hardware and software. Students will be introduced to system software and application software, learning how software enables hardware to perform useful tasks. Students will learn about operating systems, the essential software that manages all hardware and other software on a computer. This chapter covers basic functions and navigation tips. This chapter introduces the basic concepts of programming in a simple and engaging way. Through fun activities, students will develop logical thinking and problem-solving skills. We cover the use of common applications such as word processors and drawing programs. Students will learn to create and save documents, use basic editing tools, and enjoy creating their own art digitally. As students begin to explore the internet, it's crucial to teach them how to stay safe online. This chapter covers important tips on how to use the internet responsibly, avoid sharing personal information, and recognize potential online dangers. Proper computer care and etiquette are essential skills. Students will learn how to maintain their devices, use computers responsibly, and follow good practices to ensure a healthy and productive computing environment.

Our approach combines theoretical knowledge with practical activities to make learning enjoyable and effective. Each chapter includes illustrations and diagrams to help students visualize concepts, hands-on activities that reinforce learning, and review questions to assess understanding.

Table of Content

Chapter 1: Peek Inside Your Computer!

In this chapter you will learn about:

What's Inside?
The Brain (CPU)!
New Friends: Devices!

Welcome, young explorers, to a journey through the insides of a computer! This chapter, "Peek Inside Your Computer," is like a field trip to the inside of one of the coolest machines ever created. We'll learn what makes a computer work, starting from its brain (the CPU), meeting its helpful friends (devices), and understanding the special language it speaks through components. Let's get ready to become computer experts!

What's Inside?
When we look at a computer, we usually only see the outside—screen, keyboard, and mouse. But inside the case, there are many parts working together to make everything function smoothly. Let's look closer at each of these parts:

Motherboard: The motherboard is like the "central hub" of the computer. It's a large circuit board where all the parts connect and communicate. Imagine it as the computer's nervous system, with pathways that send signals between different parts.

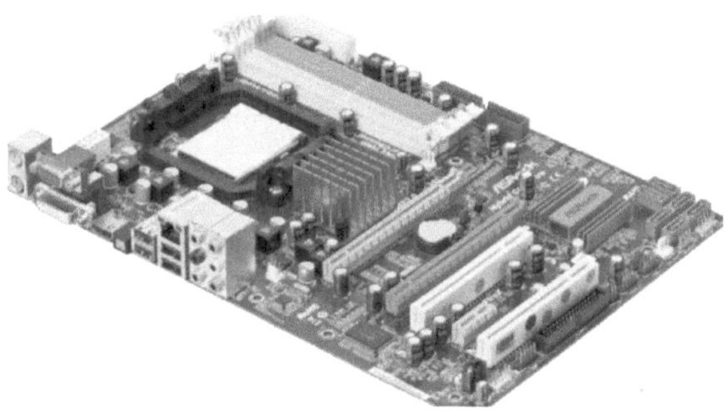

CPU Socket: The CPU (which we'll talk more about later) is connected to the motherboard through a special socket. This is where the computer's "brain" is attached.

Power Supply: The power supply gives energy to every part of the computer. It's like the heart that pumps electricity to all the other components so they can work. When you plug your computer into an outlet, it sends power to the power supply, which then distributes it to other parts safely.

RAM (Random Access Memory): This is like the computer's short-term memory. RAM temporarily stores the data and instructions that the CPU needs quickly. For example, when you're playing a game or watching a video, that data is stored in RAM so that it's easily accessible.

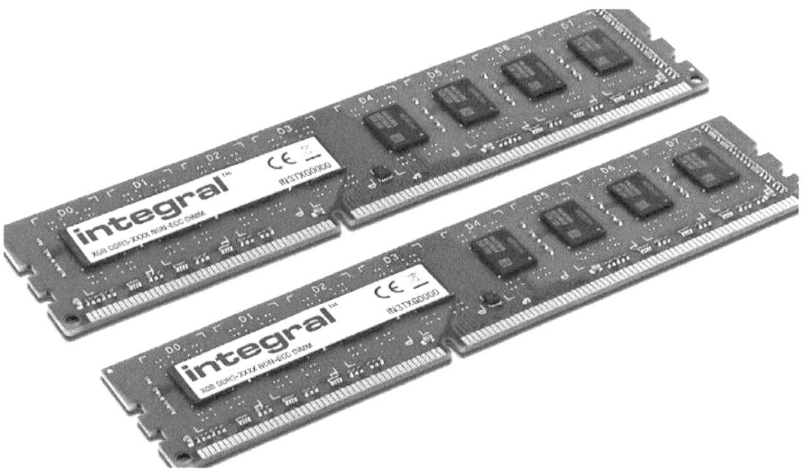

Hard Drive and SSD (Solid-State Drive): These are the storage units where the computer saves all your files, like documents, games, and photos. Hard drives have spinning disks inside that read and write data, while SSDs have no moving parts and are much faster. SSDs are like high-speed storage that makes your computer run smoothly.

Fun Fact: Did you know that the world's first hard drive was as big as a refrigerator and could hold only a tiny amount of data? Today, our smallest flash drives hold way more data than that!

The Brain (CPU)!

The CPU, or Central Processing Unit, is like the brain of the computer. It handles everything your computer does, from adding numbers to playing games. Let's dive into its different parts and how it works:

Control Unit (CU): The CU is like a director in a movie. It tells the other parts of the CPU what to do and when. Whenever you open an app or play a game, the CU is giving directions, making sure each part of the computer knows its job.

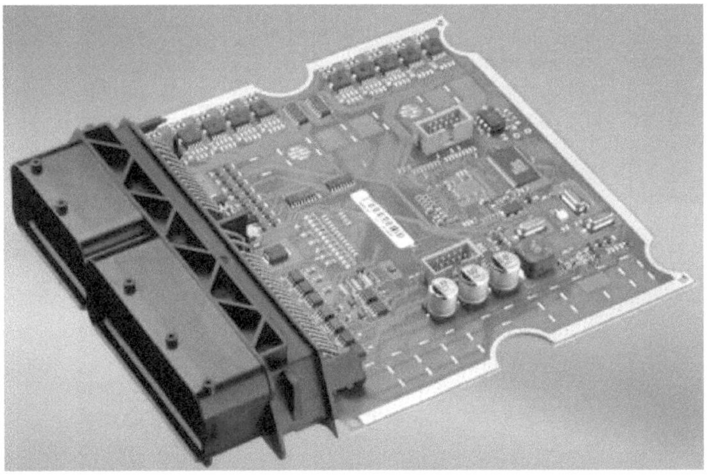

Arithmetic Logic Unit (ALU): The ALU is where all the math happens. It adds, subtracts, and makes logical comparisons. For example, if you ask the computer to add 5 + 3, the ALU is the part doing the math!

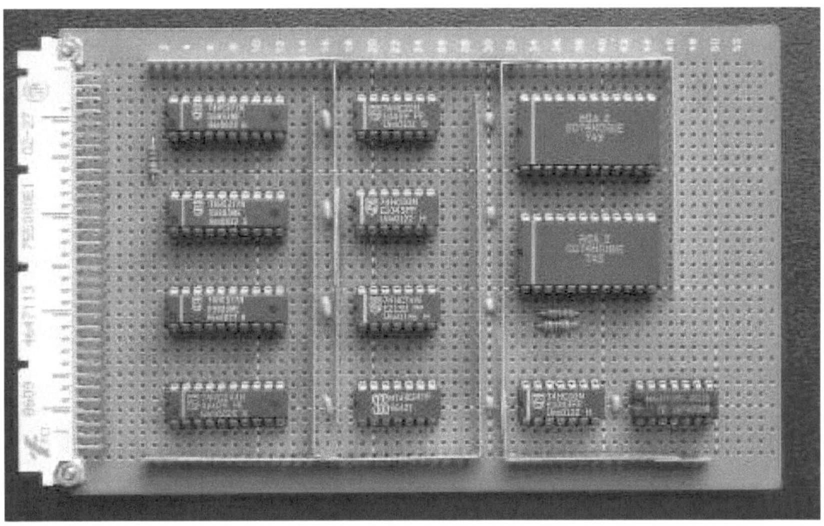

Registers: Registers are very small, fast storage areas inside the CPU. They hold data that the CPU needs to access quickly, like instructions and small bits of data for calculations.

Clock Speed: The clock speed measures how fast the CPU can carry out tasks. It's like the beat in a song—each beat is a moment when the CPU can process data. Higher clock speeds mean the CPU can process more instructions in a second, making the computer faster.

Fun Fact: A modern CPU can perform billions of instructions per second, which is faster than you could ever count!

New Friends: Devices!

Computers don't just work alone—they have friends, called devices, that make them even more useful. These devices help us interact with the computer and enjoy different activities like typing, watching videos, and listening to music.

Keyboard and Mouse: The keyboard lets you type words, while the mouse lets you point and click. They are like the computer's hands, allowing us to communicate and give commands.

Monitor: The monitor is the screen that displays what's happening inside the computer. It's like the computer's eyes, showing you everything in the form of images, text, and videos.

Printer: The printer is like a magic tool that takes things from your screen and puts them on paper. You can print pictures, documents, and even art projects to keep or share with others.

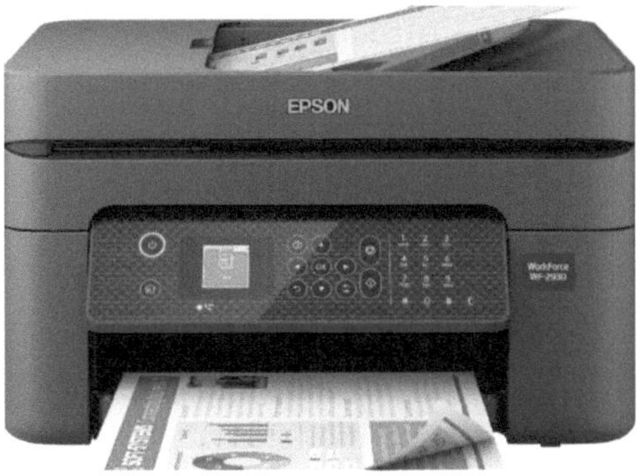

Speakers and Microphones: Speakers let you hear sounds and music from the computer, while the microphone allows you to record your voice or sounds. These are helpful for video calls, playing games with sound, or even recording music.

Scanner: A scanner lets you copy images or documents onto your computer by turning them into digital files. It's handy for saving old photos or making digital copies of important papers.

Fun Fact: The first computer mouse was invented in the 1960s and was made out of wood! Today, we have wireless mice that don't even need cords.

Glossary
Motherboard: The main circuit board that connects all parts of a computer and allows them to communicate.
CPU (Central Processing Unit): Known as the computer's brain, it processes all instructions and data.
Control Unit (CU): Part of the CPU that directs other components on what actions to take.
Arithmetic Logic Unit (ALU): The part of the CPU responsible for calculations and logic.
Clock Speed: The speed at which the CPU operates, measured in cycles per second.
RAM (Random Access Memory): Temporary memory that stores data the CPU needs to access quickly.
Hard Drive: A storage device with moving parts, used for long-term data storage.
SSD (Solid-State Drive): A faster storage device without moving parts, used for long-term data storage.
Keyboard: An input device used for typing text and numbers.
Mouse: An input device used to point, click, and interact with items on the screen.
Monitor: The screen that displays images and videos.
Printer: A device that prints images and documents from the computer onto paper.
Speakers: Output devices that produce sound from the computer.
Microphone: An input device that records sound.

Summary
Let's wrap up what we've learned with a quick summary:
Computers have many parts inside, including the motherboard, power supply, RAM, and storage devices (Hard Drive/SSD).

Known as the "brain," the CPU handles all instructions and calculations. Its parts include the Control Unit (CU) and Arithmetic Logic Unit (ALU).
Computers use many devices like the keyboard, mouse, monitor, printer, speakers, and microphone to make working and playing easier and more fun.

Exercises

Exercise 1 – Choose the correct answer
1.What part of the computer is considered the "brain" those processes instructions?
a) Monitor
b) CPU
c) Hard Drive
d) Mouse
2.Which device is used to input text into the computer?
a) Monitor
b) Printer
c) Keyboard
d) Speaker

Exercise 2 – True/False
1. The motherboard is the main circuit board where all parts of a computer are connected.
2. A scanner displays images and videos from the computer on a screen.

Exercise 3- Rearrange the sentence
1. brain / the / computer's / CPU / is / the
2. main / board / all / motherboard / the / parts / is / that / connect / circuit

Exercise 4- Choose the Odd One Out
1. Choose Odd One Out
a) Keyboard
b) Monitor
c) Printer
d) CPU
2. Choose Odd One Out
a) Hard Drive
b) SSD
c) RAM
d) Mouse

Exercise 5- Short Questions
1. Why is the CPU often called the "brain" of the computer?
2. What is the primary function of the motherboard?

Answer

Exercise 1 – 1. b) CPU, 2. c) Keyboard
Exercise 2 – 1. True, 2. False

Exercise 3 – 1. The CPU is the computer's brain.
2. The motherboard is the main circuit board that connects all parts.
Exercise 4 – 1. d) CPU, 2.d) Mouse

Project

Understand the essential components of a computer by creating a model using household materials.

Activity

Solve the Riddles:
1.I'm the part that lets you see pictures, text, and movies of glee. I show you things in colourful displays. Tell me, what am I today?
2.I'm known as the brain, though I'm not alive. I help you with tasks; I help you survive. All instructions go through me, whether small or grand. Who am I? Can you understand?

Case Study

Sarah, a 10-year-old, just received her first computer. She is excited to use it for school projects, games, and drawing.

Discussion Questions:
1.How should Sarah use her computer safely without straining her eyes?
2.What should Sarah do if her computer starts acting strange or slow?
3.Which part of the computer will Sarah use most if she wants to type a story?

Group Discussion

Discuss in the group how computers help us in daily life.

Online Interactive Resources

Online Exam Paper
Link: https://forms.gle/f6cAoXL9TRt4KvmT9

QR Code:

Chapter 1 Videos
Link: https://www.youtube.com/playlist?list=PLzlh_31VWEFqdWAShl02OggQbN9lcllBP

QR Code:

Chapter-1
Test Paper
Peek Inside Your Computer!

Time Duration: 20 Minutes **Maximum Marks: 10**

General Instructions:

1. The question paper consists of 10 questions.
2. All questions are compulsory.

True/False- **(1 X 2 = 2 marks)**

1.The CPU is also known as the "brain" of the computer.

2.The monitor is a device used to store information on the computer.

Choose the Correct Option **(1 x 3 = 3 marks)**

1. Which part of the computer displays images and text?

a) Keyboard
b) Monitor
c) Mouse
d) CPU

2. Which device is primarily used for typing letters and numbers?

a) Printer
b) Monitor
c) Keyboard
d) Speaker

3. Which part of the computer temporarily stores data while you're working on it?

a) Hard Drive
b) RAM
c) Monitor
d) Power Supply

Short Questions **(1 x 5 = 5 marks)**

1. Why is the CPU often called the "brain" of the computer?
2. What is the primary purpose of the motherboard in a computer?
3. Explain one difference between a hard drive and an SSD.
4. How does a keyboard help in interacting with a computer?
5. Name two input devices and explain their functions.

Chapter 2: Super Software Fun!

In this chapter you will learn about:
The Boss Software
Apps for Everything
Add or Remove Magic

Introduce the concept of software as the invisible "brain" of the computer that tells it what to do. Compare the hardware (physical parts) to a skeleton or machine, and software to the instructions or programs that make everything work smoothly.

What is Software?

Explain that software is a set of instructions that helps devices perform tasks. Imagine trying to build a house without a plan. Software is like a blueprint for computers and gadgets, guiding them on what to do.

Types of Software

System Software: This software includes operating systems like Windows, iOS, and Android, which manage the entire device.

Application Software (Apps): These are programs designed for specific tasks, like games, calculators, or painting tools.

Importance of Software

Software turns a device into a helpful tool, whether it's a computer, smartphone, or tablet. Without software, these devices would just sit there, unable to perform any useful tasks.

The Boss Software

Imagine your classroom. You have students, desks, books, and a teacher who ensures everyone follows the rules, listens, and learns. Without the teacher, there would be a lot of noise, and it would be hard to get anything done, right? Well, a computer has its own "teacher" called the Operating System (OS), which is the "boss" of all the other software on the computer.
The OS manages everything inside the computer or device like a teacher organises the class. Without it, all the parts and apps on your computer wouldn't know what to do.

What is an Operating System (OS)?
The Operating System (OS) is software that controls and manages the whole computer. It's the first software that starts running when you turn on your computer, and it stays running to ensure everything works smoothly.

The OS is like the "boss" of the computer, telling each part what to do, managing all the files, running apps, and keeping everything organised. It's also in charge of talking to the hardware (like the keyboard, screen, and mouse) and making sure they work together.

Why is the Operating System Called the Boss?

Imagine a company with lots of employees. If there's no boss, everyone would be doing their own thing without any coordination. The same goes for computers. The OS tells every program and part of the computer what to do and when to do it. Here's how:

Organises Files and Folders: The OS helps create, delete, and organise files, so it's easy to find things. Think of it as a librarian who keeps all the books in order.

Runs Apps: When you want to open a game or app, it's the OS that starts it up and makes sure it runs properly.

Manages Memory: Computers have a certain amount of memory to store information temporarily. The OS decides which programs can use the memory, just like a boss who decides who gets to use the meeting room.

Keeps Things Secure: The OS has security settings that protect the computer from harmful software. It's like a boss who makes sure only trusted people enter the office.

Controls Hardware: The OS makes sure all the parts of the computer, like the keyboard, mouse, and screen, work together. It's like a conductor directing all the instruments in an orchestra.

Types of Operating Systems
Different devices have different operating systems. Here are a few examples:

Windows: It is a popular operating system for many computers worldwide. You may have seen it on school or home computers.
macOS: Used on Apple computers, macOS has a unique look and is known for its simplicity.
Android: This OS is used on many smartphones and tablets. You may recognise it on your phone or tablet.
iOS: Apple devices like iPhones and iPads use iOS, which is similar to MacOS but designed for touchscreens.
Each of these operating systems does the same job of being the device's "boss" but in slightly different ways.

How Does the OS Help You Every Day?
You always interact with the OS, even if you don't realise it! Here are some things the OS helps you with every day:

Opening and Closing Apps: When you tap an app on your tablet or computer, the OS opens it and ensures it works properly.
Saving Your Work: The OS saves your files and organises them in folders so you can find them later.
Using Multiple Apps: If you switch between a game and your homework, the OS manages both without letting one crash.
Adjusting Volume and Brightness: The OS helps you change settings like sound and brightness on your device.

Did you know? The earliest operating systems were created in the 1950s. They were much simpler and could only do basic tasks. But without them, computers wouldn't be able to work like they do now.
Guess what? Operating systems are not just on computers but also in devices like smart TVs, washing machines, and even cars! These help the devices run smoothly and respond to commands.

Why is it Important to Have an Operating System?
Without an OS, you would have to tell each part of the computer what to do separately, and it would be exhausting! The OS does all the hard work of coordinating so you can focus on using your device. It makes

using computers and devices easy, organised, and efficient, allowing you to open apps, save work, and browse the internet without confusion.

Apps for Everything

Imagine if you could have a tool for everything you want to do right in your pocket or on your computer. Need help with homework? Want to play a game? Want to talk to friends or family? You can do all of this with apps! Apps are software designed for specific tasks, like learning math, playing games, or chatting with friends.

Let's dive into the world of apps and see how they make our lives easier, more fun, and even a bit more creative.

What Are Apps?

Apps (short for "applications") are like little helpers on your device, whether it's a tablet, phone, or computer. They are programs made to do specific tasks. Some are for learning, some are for fun, and others help us get organized or communicate.

Think of apps as digital tools that you can install on your devices, just like putting different tools in a toolbox.

Types of Apps

There are so many different kinds of apps! Here are a few examples to help you understand how they work and how they fit into everyday life.

Educational Apps

These apps are made for learning and are super helpful for school subjects or hobbies.

Examples: Duolingo (for learning languages), Khan Academy Kids (for learning different subjects), Prodigy Math (for fun math practice), and Google Earth (for exploring the world).

Game Apps

These apps are for fun and entertainment. They come in different types, from puzzles to action-packed adventures.

Examples: Minecraft (where you can build worlds and explore), Among Us (a detective game), and Angry Birds (a fun physics-based game).

Social Media Apps

These apps help us stay in touch with friends and family. You can share photos, videos, and messages.

Examples: WhatsApp (for chatting), Instagram (for sharing photos), and Facebook Messenger (for messaging and video calls).

Productivity Apps

These apps help us stay organized and get things done. Some apps help you plan your day, while others help you keep track of important tasks.

Examples: Google Calendar (for scheduling), Notes (for jotting down ideas), and To-Do List (for managing tasks).

Creative Apps

Creative apps let you explore your artistic side. You can draw, create music, edit photos, or make videos.

Examples: Procreate (for digital drawing), GarageBand (for making music), and Canva (for creating beautiful designs).

Why Apps are So Useful?

Apps are a big part of our lives, and they help us in many ways. Here's how:

Learning New Skills

Apps like Duolingo can help you learn a new language. Other apps, like Khan Academy, can teach you math, science, history, and much more!

Staying Connected
With messaging apps like WhatsApp, you can send texts, pictures, and even voice messages to friends and family, no matter where they are in the world.
Having Fun
Game apps like Roblox and Minecraft let you play and even connect with friends. You can build virtual worlds, go on adventures, and let your creativity shine!
Staying Organized
Apps like Google Calendar and Notes help you keep track of your schedule, homework, and even personal goals.
Creating and Sharing Art
Apps like Procreate and Canva let you draw, paint, and design. You can even make digital posters and cards to share with friends and family.

Popular Apps for Kids
Here are some apps that kids love and that are also educational:
Scratch Jr.: A simple coding app where you can create animations and stories. It's perfect for young programmers.
ABCmouse: A learning app that covers many subjects with fun activities.
YouTube Kids: A safe version of YouTube with videos on almost every topic you can imagine.
Book Creator: An app where you can create your own digital books with pictures, text, and drawings.
These apps are all about fun and learning. They let you explore new interests, from reading to art to coding!
Fun Facts About Apps
Did you know? There are over 2 million apps available in the app stores! Whether you want to learn guitar or identify stars in the night sky, there's probably an app for it.
Guess what? The most popular apps worldwide are social media and messaging apps like WhatsApp and TikTok.
Amazing! Some apps are so smart that they can use your phone's camera to identify plants and animals just by taking a picture!

How to Use Apps Safely
It's important to be smart when using apps. Here are some tips for using apps safely:
Download from Trusted Sources
Only download apps from trusted apps like the Apple App Store or Google Play Store. Avoid unknown websites that might have harmful apps.
Check Permissions
Some apps ask for permission to use your camera or microphone. Always ask an adult if you're not sure why an app needs these permissions.
Keep Your Device Clean
If you have too many apps, it might make your device run slower. Regularly uninstall apps you don't use.
Watch Out for Ads
Some apps have ads that can be annoying. Be careful not to click on ads, as they can sometimes lead to unwanted websites.

Add or Remove Magic

Imagine that your tablet or phone is like a backpack. Just like you choose what to put in your backpack – maybe a favourite book, some snacks, and a notebook – you can also choose what to put on your device. But you can't keep adding things forever, or it will get too full and hard to use.

Adding (or installing) and removing (or uninstalling) apps is like organising your backpack. You can keep the things you need and get rid of things you don't. Let's learn how adding and removing apps works and why it's like a little magic trick for your device!

What Does it Mean to Add (or Install) an App?

When you add or install an app, it means you're bringing a new tool or game onto your device, just like adding a new item to your backpack. Once the app is installed, it's ready for you to use whenever you want.

Steps to Install an App:

Go to the App Store: Most devices like the Apple App Store **or** Google Play Store have an app **store**. This is where you find new apps to add.

Search for an App: Type in the name of the app you want, like a drawing app or a math game.

Download and Install: Click on the download button. The device will install the app, which means it's putting it on your device and getting it ready for use.

Open and Enjoy: Once installed, you can open the app and start using it!

Fun Fact: Did you know? Some apps are free, but some cost money. Free apps might have ads or in-app purchases, so always ask an adult if you're unsure.

What Does it Mean to Remove (or Uninstall) an App?

Removing or uninstalling an app means removing it from your device. Maybe you no longer need it, or maybe you need more space for other apps. Uninstalling an app is like cleaning out your backpack—it makes more room and keeps things organised.

Steps to Uninstall an App:

Find the App: Look for the app you want to remove on your home screen or app list.

Press and Hold: Press the app icon until options appear.

Select 'Uninstall' or 'Delete': Choose the option to remove the app. Some devices ask you to confirm.

Space Cleared!: Now, the app is gone, and you have extra space on your device.

Why Is It Important to Manage Your Apps?

Managing your apps helps your device stay organised and work faster. Here's why it matters:

Saves Storage Space

Each app you install takes up a little space. If you have too many apps, your device can get "full," making it run slowly. Removing apps you don't use makes space for new ones.

Keeps Your Device Fast

When you have too many apps, your device has to work harder, which can make it slow down. Uninstalling unused apps gives your device a "breather."

Protects Your Device

Some apps can contain harmful software (malware), especially from unknown sources. It's always safest to only download apps from the app store and remove apps that look suspicious.

Organize your Screen

Having fewer apps on your home screen means you can easily find the ones you use the most.

App Permissions: What Are They and Why Do They Matter?

When you install an app, it may ask for certain permissions. Permissions allow the app to use parts of your device, like the camera, microphone, or location. Some apps need these permissions to work properly (like a photo app needing access to your camera).

Tips for Managing Permissions:

Only Allow Necessary Permissions: Don't allow an app that doesn't need access to something. For example, a calculator app doesn't need your camera.
Ask an Adult: If you're unsure why an app needs permission, ask an adult.
Check Settings: You can see and change app permissions in your device's settings.
Fun Fact: Some apps ask for funny permissions that don't make sense! Always be cautious and check with an adult if you're unsure.

How to Keep Your Device Safe with Apps
When adding or removing apps, it's important to keep your device safe:
Download from Trusted Sources
Only use the official app store to download apps. Unknown websites can have harmful apps.
Be Careful with Free Apps
Free apps can sometimes come with ads or "in-app purchases." Be careful not to click on ads, and always ask before purchasing.
Update Your Apps
Updates make sure apps work well and stay secure. Regularly updating apps helps keep your device safe and apps running smoothly.

Fun Facts About Installing and Removing Apps
Did you know? If your device gets full, you can sometimes save space by moving photos and videos to cloud storage instead of uninstalling your favourite apps!
Cool Tip! Some apps, like photo editing or game apps, occupy more space than others. If you're low on space, try deleting larger apps first.
Interesting Fact! Apps can be updated automatically to improve performance and security. Updates are like "mini upgrades" that keep apps fresh.

Why Managing Apps is Like Magic
Managing apps gives you control over what's on your device. You decide what stays, what goes, and what gets updated—it's like having a magic wand for your tablet or phone!
Add Magic: When you install an app, you add new tools and games that make your device more fun and useful.
Remove Magic: When you uninstall an app, you make more space and keep your device running smoothly.

Glossary
Operating System (OS): Software that controls the entire computer or device and helps it run smoothly.
Application (App): A program designed for a specific task, like a game, calculator, or drawing tool.
Download: Copying data or software from the internet to a device.
Install: Set up software on a device to be ready for use.
Uninstall: Removing software from a device.
Permissions: Settings allow apps to access a device's features, like the camera or location.
Malware: Harmful software that can damage a device or steal information.

Summary
Software makes devices worthwhile, allowing them to perform various tasks.
The Operating System (OS) is the leading software that manages all other software and hardware on a device.
Applications (Apps) let us play games, learn, and be creative.
We can install and remove apps to customize our devices and make space.
App permissions should be managed carefully to keep devices safe.
Managing apps wisely helps devices work better and prevents unwanted software.

Exercises

Exercise 1 – Choose the correct answer

1. Which of the following is known as the "boss" software that manages all other programs on a device
a) Game App
b) Operating System
c) Calculator
d) Music Player
2. Which type of app would you use to learn a new language?
a) Social Media App
b) Gaming App
c) Educational App
d) Photo Editing App

Exercise 2 – True/False

1.The Operating System controls hardware like the keyboard and mouse.
2.Uninstalling apps you don't need helps keep your device running smoothly.

Exercise 3- Rearrange the sentence

1.devices / help / apps / us / different / with / tasks.
2.system / the / boss / operating / is / the / of / computer.

Exercise 4- Choose the Odd One Out

1.Choose the odd one: a) Windows, b) macOS, c) Android, d) Minecraft
2.Choose the odd one: a) Drawing App, b) Messaging App, c) Calendar App, d) Operating System

Exercise 8- Short Questions

1.Why is it important to only download apps from trusted sources?
2.What is the role of an operating system on a device?

Answer

Exercise 1- 1. b) Operating System, 2. c) Educational App
Exercise 2- 1. True, 2. True
Exercise 3- 1. Apps help us with different tasks on devices.
2. The operating system is the boss of the computer.
Exercise 4- 1. d) Minecraft, 2. d) Operating System

Project

Create a poster or booklet titled "My App World," where we will explore different types of apps, their uses, and why they are useful.

Activity

1.I help you find places near and far, follow my maps, whether by bike or car.

What app am I?

2.I let you chat, call, and share, Pictures and messages sent with care.
What app am I?
3.I'm full of numbers, shapes, and more; with games and quizzes, I make learning not a bore.
What app am I?
4.With just a swipe, you can snap a shot, share your pictures, and edit a lot.
What app am I?
5.When it's time to get creative and draw, I'm the app you use without a flaw.
What app am I?

Case Study

Ava is a 10-year-old who loves using her tablet to learn and play games. She recently downloaded many new apps, but now her tablet runs very slowly, and she keeps seeing ads pop up. Some apps even ask for permission to access her camera and microphone, but Ava doesn't know if she should allow them or not.

Discussion Questions:

1.What do you think is causing Ava's tablet to slow down?
2.How can Ava decide which apps to keep and which ones to delete?
3.Should Ava allow apps to use her camera and microphone? Why or why not?
4.What advice would you give Ava to help her manage her tablet better?

Group Discussion

Share opinions on apps and practice critical thinking about how and when to use them.

Online Interactive Resources

Online Exam Paper
Link: https://forms.gle/GR2mAFEMQJJWBsAq7

QR Code:

Chapter 2 Videos
Link: https://www.youtube.com/playlist?list=PLzlh_31VWEFoAZ1a0GG-azEtAYI-ea3rY

QR Code:

Chapter-2
Test Paper
Super Software Fun!

Time Duration: 20 Minutes **Maximum Marks: 10**

General Instructions:
1. The question paper consists of 10 questions.
2. All questions are compulsory.

SECTION-A

True/False- **(1 X 2 = 2 marks)**
1. An operating system is necessary for a computer to run other applications.
2. Uninstalling unused apps can help make your device run faster.

Choose the Correct Option **(1 X 3 = 3 marks)**
1. Which of these is an example of an educational app?
a) Instagram
b) Duolingo
c) Angry Birds
d)WhatsApp
2. What does an operating system do?
a) Only plays music
b) Manages all other software on the device
c) Draws pictures
d) Sends messages
3. Which type of app would you use to organise your daily tasks?
a) Calendar app
b) Game app
c) Music app
d) Social media app

Short Questions **(1 X 5 = 5 marks)**
1.What is the role of an operating system on a device?
2.Why should we only download apps from trusted sources?
3.Explain one reason why it's good to uninstall apps you no longer use.
4.Name two types of apps and describe what each one does.
5.How can an app like Duolingo be helpful for students?

Chapter 3: Excel Wonders!

In this chapter, you will learn about:

Tables Made Easy!
Click and Link!
Basic Formulae in Excel

In this chapter, we'll explore how Excel can help us organize and manage data like a pro. Excel is a powerful tool for creating tables, linking information, and performing calculations with just a few clicks. Each topic will guide you through fun and easy-to-follow steps to get comfortable with Excel. Let's dive in and discover the wonders of Excel together!

Tables Made Easy!

What is a Table?

Tables in Excel are a way of arranging data in rows and columns. This layout helps make data easier to read, understand, and analyze. A table is made up of cells, each identified by a unique address like A1, B2, etc.

Creating a Table in Excel

Step 1: Select the cells you want to turn into a table.
Step 2: Go to the "Insert" tab, then click on "Table."
Step 3: Check if your table has headers (titles for each column), then click "OK."
Result: Excel will automatically format your selection into a table.

Using Table Styles

Tables can be styled with colors to make them more appealing. Using the "Table Styles" option in Excel, students can apply a variety of colors and designs.

Step 1: Select your table.
Step 2: Go to the "Table Design" tab.
Step 3: Choose a style that suits your table's theme.

Sorting and Filtering Data

Sorting and filtering help manage large sets of data. For example, sorting can arrange grades from highest to lowest, while filtering can show only specific grades.

Step 1: Select your table.
Step 2: Click on the column header to sort or apply a filter.

Fun Fact: Excel tables can automatically expand! If you start typing below the table, Excel includes the new row automatically.

Click and Link!

Hyperlinks in Excel

Hyperlinks in Excel are shortcuts to other places, like websites, other sheets, or documents. They help connect different parts of your workbook for easy navigation.

Creating a Hyperlink:

Step 1: Select a cell where you want the link.
Step 2: Right-click and choose "Link."
Step 3: Choose "Existing File or Web Page," enter the link, and press "OK."

Linking Cells
Cell linking lets one cell reflect the value of another, which is great for creating summaries or totals.
Step 1: Click on the cell you want to link.
Step 2: Type "=" and select the cell you want to link to.
Step 3: Press "Enter," and your cell will now show the linked value.

Linking Data Across Sheets
Linking across sheets can combine information from multiple sheets.
Fun Fact: Linking cells can be used for anything! Some businesses use this to update prices automatically across spreadsheets.

Basic Formulae in Excel

Exploring the Excel Window
Understanding the layout: Excel is made up of rows and columns forming cells. Each cell has a unique address, like "B3."
Tabs in Excel, such as "Home," "Insert," and "Data," offer different tools for working with data.

Entering and Formatting Text
Students will learn how to enter text and numbers, format font size, color, and style to make their data look good.

Simple Formulas and Functions
Excel functions perform calculations. Introduce SUM, AVERAGE, and COUNT.
Example: To sum up hours studied:
Step 1: Click on the cell where you want the result.
Step 2: Type =SUM(B2) to add up the hours listed in cells B2 to B5.

Using the Autofill Tool
Autofill helps complete series quickly, like numbers or dates.
Fun Fact: The average Excel user only uses about 10% of its total features, but that 10% covers most everyday needs!

Glossary

Cell: A single box in an Excel worksheet where data is entered.
Row: A horizontal line of cells in Excel, labeled with numbers.
Column: A vertical line of cells in Excel, labeled with letters.
Table: A structured format in Excel for organizing data, which makes it easy to read and sort.
Formula: A way to perform calculations in Excel by typing an equal sign followed by the function.
Hyperlink: A clickable link that takes you to another place in Excel or on the internet.
Linking Cells: A way to connect cells so changes in one reflect in another.
Autofill: A tool in Excel that helps fill in cells automatically when it detects a pattern.
SUM Function: An Excel function used to add numbers in a range of cells.

Summary

Tables in Excel help organize data and make it easy to read and analyse. Students learned to create tables, apply styles, sort, and filter data.
Hyperlinks and Links make Excel interactive. Hyperlinks link to websites, files, or sheets, while cell links connect data across the workbook.
Basic Functions in Excel include SUM, AVERAGE, and COUNT, which make it easy to perform calculations.
Autofill saves time by automatically completing patterns, like dates or sequences.

Exercises

Exercise 1 – Choose the correct answer

1. Which of the following is the correct way to start a formula in Excel?
A) /
B) @
C) =
D) #
2. What is the main purpose of a table in Excel?
A) To add pictures
B) To organize data
C) To create animations
D) To insert videos

Exercise 2 – True/False

1. A cell address in Excel is identified by a combination of a letter (for the column) and a number (for the row).
2. Hyperlinks in Excel can only be used to link to websites, not to other sheets.

Exercise 3- Rearrange the sentence

1. Excel / used / for / data / organizing / is / tables / in.
2. calculations / perform / in / we / formulas / with / Excel.

Exercise 4- Choose the Odd One Out

1. Which one is different?
A) Row
B) Column
C) Table
D) Slide
2. Which one doesn't belong in Excel?
A) Cell
B) WordArt
C) Hyperlink
D) Sheet

Exercise 5- Short Questions

1. What is the purpose of the "Autofill" tool in Excel?
2. How can you create a hyperlink to another worksheet in the same Excel file?

Answers

Exercise 1- 1. C) =, 2. B) To organize data
Exercise 2: 1. True, 2. False
Exercise 3: 1. Excel is used for organizing data in tables., 2. We perform calculations with formulas in Excel.
Exercise 4: 1. D) Slide, 2. B) WordArt

Project

Organize information in a table format using Excel about the collection of toys in your cupboard.

Activity

1."I'm a little box, tiny and square, With letters and numbers, I'm always there. When you enter data, I hold it tight, Find me in rows and columns, I'm just right!
What am I?"
2."I'm the tool to help you out, Adding things without a doubt. Just type me in and I'll give you a sum, Numbers together, here I come!
What am I?"

Case Study

Imagine your class went on a trip to the zoo. Your teacher asked you to help create a report with details about the animals you saw, where they are from, and some interesting facts.

Discussion Questions:
1.Why is it helpful to use a table when you have lots of information?
2.If you had to tell a friend about your zoo trip, would the table make it easier to remember details? How?
3.Which animal was your favuorite and why?

Group Discussion

Discuss in group how we can apply excel in daily life.

Online Interactive Resources

Online Exam Paper
Link: https://forms.gle/unbDoeVZ9uWNGc8f8

QR Code:

Chapter 3 Videos
Link: https://www.youtube.com/playlist?list=PLzlh_31VWEFoH9vrau4kPh1pUWLlzTAgy

QR Code:

Chapter-3
Test Paper
Excel Wonders!

Time Duration: 20 Minutes **Maximum Marks: 10**

General Instructions:
1. The question paper consists of 10 questions.
2. All questions are compulsory.

True/False- **(1 X 2 = 2 marks)**

1. Excel is used only for drawing pictures. (True/False)
2. In Excel, a formula always begins with an equal sign (=). (True/False)

Choose the Correct Option – **(1 X 3 = 3 marks)**

1. What is a cell in Excel?
A) A document
B) A small box to store data
C) A large file
D) A design template

2. Which of the following is a way to add numbers in Excel?
A) Filter
B) Hyperlink
C) SUM function
D) Table

3. What feature allows you to fill cells with a pattern or series in Excel?
A) Autofill
B) Hyperlink
C) Filter
D) Table

Short Questions – **(1 X 5 = 5 marks)**

1.What is the main purpose of using tables in Excel?
2.How can you create a new row in an Excel table?
3.Why is sorting data helpful in Excel?
4.What symbol is used to start a formula in Excel?
5.Name one tool in Excel that helps you organize large amounts of information.

Half Yearly Test Paper

Time Duration: 40 Minutes **Maximum Marks: 30**

General Instructions:

1. The question paper consists of 25 questions and is divided into four sections, A and B.
2. All questions are compulsory.
3. Section A comprises True/False, Fill in the blanks and one word of one mark each.
4. Section B comprises question numbers 1 to 5. These are short questions that carry two marks each.

SECTION-A

Fill in the blanks- **(1 X 10 = 10marks)**

1. The main part of the computer that processes data is called the ______.
2. Devices like a printer and scanner are known as ______ devices.
3. The software that manages the computer's resources is called the ______.
4. ______ is the shortcut used to copy selected text or data.
5. The ______ is known as the "brain" of the computer.
6. In Excel, a box where you enter data is called a ______.
7. ______ are small programs or tools that let you perform tasks like writing or drawing.
8. The CPU is often compared to a human ______.
9. To add more storage, you might connect an external ______ to your computer.
10. In Excel, to link one cell to another, we use ______.

True/False – **(1 X 5 = 5 marks)**

1. The CPU is the only hardware component in a computer. (True/False)
2. Applications like games and writing tools are types of software. (True/False)
3. A keyboard is an example of output hardware. (True/False)
4. The operating system controls all other software on a computer. (True/False)
5. Excel is used to create presentations. (True/False)

One Word – **(1 X 5 = 5 marks)**

1. Name the main device responsible for processing information in a computer.
2. What type of software helps us perform specific tasks, like drawing or typing?
3. What is a computer's main storage device called?
4. Which function in Excel helps add numbers quickly?
5. Name the device used to display information visually.

SECTION-B

Short Question- **(2 X 5 = 10 marks)**

1. Explain the role of the CPU in a computer.
2. What are the differences between hardware and software? Give examples of each.
3. Why is the operating system important for a computer?
4. What is the purpose of tables in Excel, and how can they be useful?
5. Name two devices that are considered both input and output devices. Explain why.

Chapter 4: Present and Protect!

In this chapter you will learn about:

Understand the Purpose of PowerPoint
Create and Organize Slides
Apply Effective Design Principles
Add Animations
Understand Online Safety Practices
Demonstrate Responsible Online Behaviour
Practice Safe Social Media Use

Wow with PowerPoint!

What is PowerPoint?

PowerPoint is a popular program used to create slideshows, or "presentations," on a computer. It's often used in schools, offices, and even for personal projects. Think of it as a tool to tell a story or explain a topic using a series of slides that combine text, images, colours, and even animations.

Why use PowerPoint?

Creating a PowerPoint presentation allows you to share information interestingly. PowerPoint makes it easier for your audience to understand and remember what you're saying, whether presenting on your favourite animal, a school project, or even a book report.

Getting started: How to create your first PowerPoint presentation

Open PowerPoint:

Begin by opening the PowerPoint program on your computer.

You'll see a blank slide or a screen with template options. Templates are pre-made designs that can make your presentation look polished and professional.

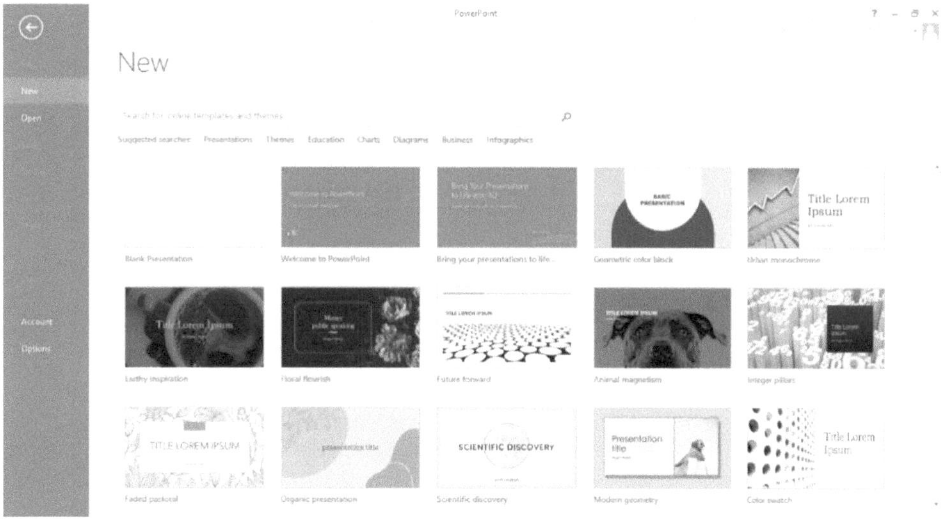

Choose a Theme or Background:

Themes are styles with colours, fonts, and backgrounds that make your presentation look cohesive. Pick a theme that suits your topic. For example, if you're presenting on a nature topic, choose a theme with green or earthy colours.

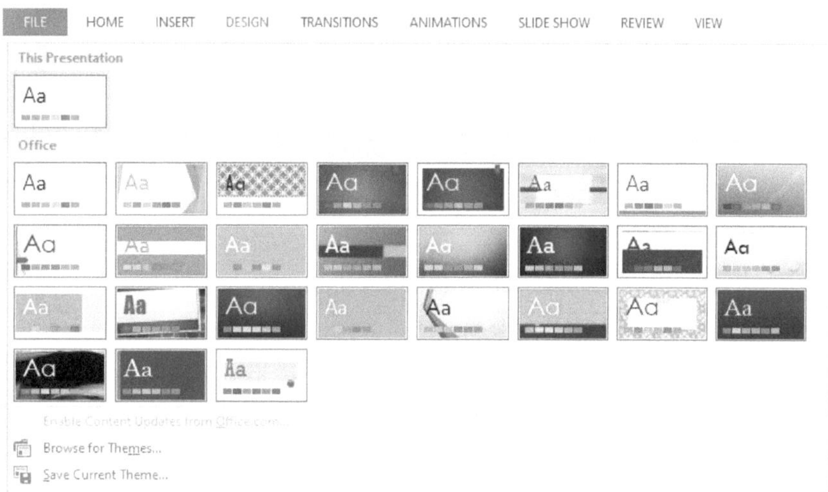

Add Slides:

Click on "New Slide" in the toolbar to add a new slide for each part of your presentation. Each slide should cover one main idea, making it easier for your audience to follow along.

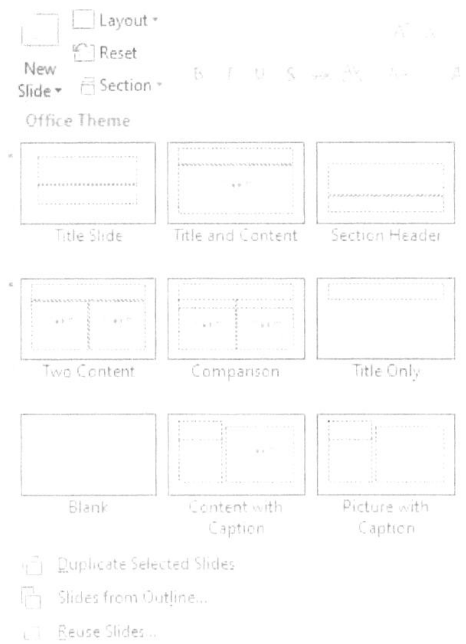

Add Text:

Each slide has a title box and a text box. Click inside these boxes to type.

In the title box, write a short, catchy title that introduces the topic of that slide. In the text box, add points or sentences to explain your idea.

Use **bullet points** for crucial points to keep it simple and organised. For example:

Lions are large cats.
They live in groups called prides.
Lions are known as the king of the jungle.

Click to add title

Click to add subtitle

Insert Images and Shapes:

To make your slides more interesting, click "Insert tab" and click "Pictures" to add an image. You can upload one from your computer or find a picture online.

You can add **shapes** (like circles, stars, or arrows) to highlight information or create simple diagrams.

Organise your content:

Arrange each slide to show one main idea. Here's a possible layout:

Slide 1: Title and Introduction – Introduce your topic.
Slide 2: Key Points – Explain your main ideas.
Slide 3: Conclusion – Summarize your main points.

Design tips to wow your audience

Keep it simple:
Avoid putting too much text on one slide. Aim for short sentences or keywords so your audience can read quickly.
Each slide should have enough "white space" (empty areas) to make it easy on the eyes.
Choose easy-to-read fonts:
Choose easy-to-read fonts, such as Arial or Calibri. Avoid using too many different fonts, as they can look messy.
Ensure the font size is large enough to read, even from a distance.
Use colours wisely:
Choose colours that match your theme but don't overwhelm the text.
Dark text on a light background or light text on a dark background is most accessible to read.
Balance Text and Images:
Include visuals that relate to your topic, but make sure they don't overpower the slide. If you're using an image, add a few short points beside it instead of filling the slide with text.

Practice Activity

To get started, create a 3-slide PowerPoint presentation about one of your favourite topics. Here's an outline you can follow:

Slide 1: Title slide – Write the title of your presentation (like "About Lions") and your name.
Slide 2: Main information – List a few interesting facts or details about your topic.
Slide 3: Conclusion – Wrap up your presentation with a summary or an interesting final fact.

Try adding at least one image and choose a simple, colourful theme. Once you're done, practice showing your presentation to a friend or family member and see if they can understand your topic by looking at your slides.

Animate Your Slides

What is Animation in PowerPoint?

Animation in PowerPoint is a feature that lets you add movement and effects to objects on your slide, such as text, images, or shapes. It can make your presentation more exciting and help highlight key points. Animations are handy for keeping your audience focused or making certain parts of your slide stand out.

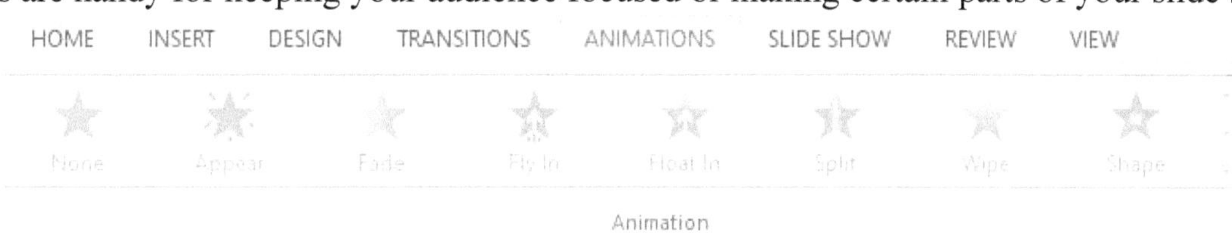

Why Use Animations?

Animations add life to your slides and help guide your audience's attention. By adding movement, you can:
Make your presentation more engaging.
Emphasise important information.
Control the flow of information, showing points one at a time instead of all at once.

Types of Animations and How to use them
PowerPoint offers different animations to apply to various objects on your slide. Here are some basic types and how they work:
Entrance Effects:
These make an object appear on the slide in creative ways. For example, text can "fly in" from the side or "fade in" gradually.
Examples: Fade In, Fly In, Zoom, etc.
When to use: Entrance effects are significant for introducing new points or showing images individually.

Emphasis Effects:
These animations draw attention to objects already on the slide and make them stand out by adding a pulse, spin, or colour change.
Examples: Spin, Pulse, Grow/Shrink, etc.
When to use: Use emphasis effects to highlight an important point or make an object stand out.

Exit Effects:
These effects make objects leave the slide, such as "fade out" or "fly out." It helps clear away information as you move to the next slide or point.
Examples: Fade Out, Fly Out, Disappear, etc.
When to use: Exit effects help remove information to keep the slide clear and direct the audience's focus to the next point.

Motion Paths:
Motion paths let you set a path for an object to follow on the slide, like moving an image from one part of the screen to another.
Examples: Line, Curve, Circle, etc.
When to use: Motion paths can show the movement or direction of a process or idea. For example, an arrow moving along a line shows progress.

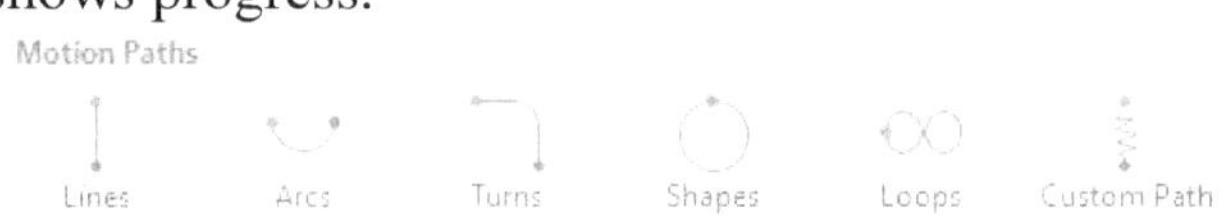

How to add Animation to your slides
Here's a step-by-step guide on how to add animations to your PowerPoint slides:
Select an Object:
Click on the text, image, or shape you want to animate.
Go to the Animations tab:
Click on the **Animations** tab at the top of your screen. This will open a menu with different animation effects.

Choose an Animation Effect:
Select an animation like Fly In or Fade. You'll see a preview of how it looks on your slide.
Customise the Effect:
Click on **Effect options** to adjust the animation's direction, speed, or style. For example, you could make the text fly in from the left or fade in from the bottom.
You can also set the **timing** to control when the animation happens automatically or when you click.
Add multiple Animations:
You can add more than one Animation to an object. For example, text can fly in (Entrance) and then spin (Emphasis) after it's on the slide. Just click **Add Animation to Layer Effects**.

Tips for using Animation effectively
While animations are fun, too many can confuse or distract your presentation. Here are some tips for making animations look professional and effective:
Use Animation sparingly:
Use animations only on key points or images. Too many moving objects can distract your audience and take away from your message.
Choose the right timing:
Timing is important. Set your animations to start "On Click" so you can control when each effect happens during your presentation. This helps you pace the information.
Keep it consistent:
Try using similar animations throughout your presentation for a clean, unified look. For instance, if you use "Fade In" for titles, use the same effect for all titles in the presentation.
Practice with the Animation pane:
The Animation Pane (in the Animations tab) shows all the animations you've added and lets you control their order. Use it to make adjustments and ensure the smooth flow of your presentation.

Practice activity

To practice your animation skills, create a simple 3-slide presentation on a topic of your choice. Try these steps:
Slide 1: Add an **Entrance Effect** like "Fly In" for your title.
Slide 2: Add **Emphasis Effects** to highlight key points (like "Pulse" or "Spin").
Slide 3: Use an **Exit Effect** to make text or an image disappear, like "Fade Out", etc.

After creating your animations, practice clicking through your slides to see how each effect looks.

Be Safe Online!

Why is Online Safety important?
The internet is a fantastic place to learn new things, play games, and connect with friends and family. But just like in the real world, following rules is essential to stay safe. Practising online safety helps protect you from risks like cyberbullying, scams, and strangers who may not have good intentions.
When you understand how to stay safe online, you can enjoy the internet while protecting yourself and your information.

Essential Online Safety rules

Here are some basic guidelines every young internet user should follow to stay safe:

Keep personal information private:

Don't share your full name, address, phone number, or school details online. This information is private and should only be shared with people you trust.

If a website or person online asks for personal details, ask a parent or teacher before sharing anything.

Create strong passwords:

Passwords are like locks that protect your online accounts. A strong password should include letters, numbers, and symbols. For example, instead of "password123," you might create something like "St@rG@laxy!9."

Never share your passwords with anyone except your parents or a trusted adult.

Be careful when talking to strangers:

Only talk to people you know online, like friends from school or family members.

If someone you don't know tries to chat or send you messages, do not respond. Let a trusted adult know if you feel uncomfortable or unsure about anyone online.

Think before you click:

Links, downloads, and ads can sometimes be traps for viruses or scams. If you see something suspicious, like a pop-up claiming you've won a prize, avoid clicking on it.

Before clicking any link or downloading a file, double-check with a parent or teacher to ensure its safety.

Tell an adult if you feel uncomfortable:

Tell an adult immediately if you see something online that makes you feel scared, sad, or confused. Don't keep it to yourself – trusted adults can help you figure out what to do.

Being a good Digital Citizen

Just as there are manners in the real world, there are also manners and responsibilities for being online. Here's how to practice being a good digital citizen:

Think before you post:

Everything you post online can stay there long, even if you delete it. Before sharing a photo, comment, or message, ask yourself if it's something you'd want everyone to see.

Only post things that are kind, respectful, and don't hurt anyone's feelings.

Respect others' privacy:

Please don't share personal information or photos of others without their permission. Like you wouldn't want your secrets shared, respect other people's privacy too.

Avoid spreading rumours:

Don't share information that might not be true or could hurt someone. If you're unsure something is true, it's better not to post or share it.

Be kind and respectful:

Treat people online the way you'd like to be treated. Avoid saying anything hurtful, and don't engage in arguments or bullying online.

Tips for safe social media use

If you're using social media or online messaging platforms, here are some additional tips:

Use Privacy Settings:

Most social media apps have privacy settings that let you control who can see your posts. Ask a parent to help you set up these settings to keep your account private.

Limit Screen Time:

Spending too much time online isn't healthy. Set limits on your screen time and make time for other activities like reading, sports, and spending time with friends in real life.

Watch Out for Fake Profiles:

Some people create fake profiles on social media. Be cautious about adding or accepting friend requests from people you don't know. If someone you don't recognise tries to connect, it's safest to ignore them.

Practice activity

To help remember these safety tips, try this activity:

Create a poster: Make a poster that includes five online safety rules that are important to you. Use markers or crayons to make it colourful and eye-catching. Hang it up near your computer or share it with your class to remind everyone of the importance of online safety.

Discuss with family or friends: Talk with a friend or family member about online safety. Share what you've learned and ask them if they have any additional tips or experiences.

Remember: Online Safety is about protecting yourself

Following these rules helps you use the internet wisely and safely. It's important to enjoy everything the online world offers while being careful and responsible. Online safety is like a shield – it helps you explore, learn, and have fun with confidence!

Summary

PowerPoint is a tool used to create engaging presentations combining text, images, and animations on slides.

Students learned how to create and organize slides using themes, titles, text, images, and shapes to present ideas clearly.

Effective design principles, like keeping slides simple, choosing readable fonts, and balancing text with images, enhance presentation quality.

Animations add movement and emphasis to slides, making presentations more dynamic and helping to control the flow of information.

Online safety practices are essential for protecting personal information and interacting safely on the internet.

Responsible digital citizenship involves thinking before posting, respecting others' privacy, and practicing kindness online.

Safe social media tips, such as using privacy settings, limiting screen time, and identifying fake profiles, help ensure a secure and positive online experience.

Glossary

PowerPoint: A program for creating presentations with slides containing text, images, and animations.
Slide: A single page in a PowerPoint presentation.
Animation: Movement effects added to slide objects like text or images.
Digital Citizen: Someone who uses the internet responsibly and respectfully.
Privacy Settings: Controls on who can see your information and activity online.
Strong Password: A secure password with a mix of letters, numbers, and symbols.
Personal Information: Details that identify a person, like name and address.

Exercises

Exercise 1 – Choose the correct answer from the given options.

1. What is the main purpose of using PowerPoint?
a. To browse the internet
b. To create presentations with slides
c. To play games
d. To write emails

2. Which of the following is a good practice for online safety?
a. Sharing your personal information freely
b. Using simple passwords
c. Respecting others' privacy and using strong passwords
d. Ignoring privacy settings

Exercise 2 – Check if the sentence is true or false.

1. Templates in PowerPoint are pre-designed layouts that help make presentations look professional.
2. Sharing your address and school name on social media is a safe practice.

Exercise 3- Fill the blank space with the correct word.

1. _______ in PowerPoint is a feature that adds movement to objects like text or images on a slide.
2. Keeping personal information private online helps ensure _______.

Exercise 4- Read the following assertion and reason carefully and choose the correct option.

1. Assertion: PowerPoint presentations help make information more engaging.
Reason: PowerPoint allows users to add images, animations, and text to slides.
a) Both Assertion and Reason are true, and Reason is the correct explanation of Assertion.
b) Both Assertion and Reason are true, but Reason is not the correct explanation of Assertion.
c) Assertion is true, but Reason is false.
d) Assertion is false, but Reason is true.

2. Assertion: A strong password should include a mix of letters, numbers, and symbols.
Reason: Strong passwords are harder to guess and provide better online security.
a) Both Assertion and Reason are true, and Reason is the correct explanation of Assertion.
b) Both Assertion and Reason are true, but Reason is not the correct explanation of Assertion.
c) Assertion is true, but Reason is false.
d) Assertion is false, but Reason is true.

Exercise 5- Short answer types of question.
1. Why is it essential to use animations sparingly in PowerPoint presentations?
2. What is the role of privacy settings on social media?
3. Explain the term "Digital Citizen."

Answer

Exercise 1- 1. b) 2. c)
Exercise 2- 1. True 2. False
Exercise 3- 1. Animation 2. Safety
Exercise 4- 1. a) 2. a)

Project

Project Title: Creating a Digital Safety Awareness Presentation
Objective:
To create a PowerPoint presentation educating classmates about the importance of online safety, covering topics like strong passwords, privacy, and responsible digital citizenship.

Instructions:
Research online safety practices that are important for young internet users.
Create a 5-slide PowerPoint presentation with the following slides:
Slide 1: Title and Introduction to Online Safety
Slide 2: The Importance of Keeping Personal Information Private
Slide 3: How to Create Strong Passwords
Slide 4: Tips for Safe Social Media Use
Slide 5: Being a Responsible Digital Citizen
Add images and animations to make the presentation engaging.
Present the slides to classmates or family members and get their feedback.

Activity

Activity Title: Online Safety Bingo
Objective:

To reinforce online safety rules fun and interactive while testing students' knowledge of best practices for staying safe on the internet.
Instructions:

Create Bingo Cards: Each student gets a Bingo card with different online safety tips and terms in each square. Examples of items could include:
Use a Strong Password
Don't Share Personal Information
Set Privacy Settings
Think Before You Post
Report Suspicious Messages
Avoid Talking to Strangers Online

Teacher's Role: The teacher reads out scenarios or statements about online safety, and students mark off the relevant squares on their Bingo cards if they have them. For example:
Arya decides to use her favourite pet's name as a password. Is this a strong password?
Ravi sees a pop-up saying he won a prize and clicks on it. What should he have done instead?

Winning the Game: Students shout "Bingo!" when they've marked off a row, column, or diagonal of correct answers.

Bonus Round:
After Bingo, students can discuss the scenarios in small groups, sharing their actions in each situation and reinforcing the online safety tips learned.

Materials Needed:
Pre-made Bingo cards with online safety tips
Markers or small tokens for students to cover their squares
This activity makes learning about online safety enjoyable and encourages students to apply their knowledge in real-life scenarios while having fun.

Case Study

Keeping Personal Information Safe Online
Scenario: Arya, a 10-year-old student, has recently started using a social media app to connect with her friends. She enjoys sharing photos of her activities and updates about her day. One day, she receives a message from someone she doesn't know, asking her for her school name and home address. Arya feels a bit uncomfortable but is unsure how to respond.

Discussion Questions:
What should Arya do in this situation to stay safe online?
How can Arya adjust her privacy settings to control who can see her posts?
Why is it essential for Arya to keep her personal information private on social media?

Group Discussion

The importance of strong passwords and online safety for students

Objective:

To help students understand the role of strong passwords in protecting personal information and accounts online, and to discuss safe online practices they can adopt.

Online Interactive Resources

Online Exam Paper

Link: https://forms.gle/SsWyd2hrxArjX6nAA

QR Code:

Chapter 4 Videos

Link: https://www.youtube.com/playlist?list=PLzlh_31VWEFqlX3XUElYxtzr5WjoMlxjv

QR Code:

Chapter-4
Test Paper
Present and Protect!

Time Duration: 20 Minutes **Maximum Marks: 10**

General Instructions:

1. The question paper consists of 10 questions.
2. All questions are compulsory.

SECTION-A

Check if the sentence is true or false. **(1 X 2 = 2 marks)**

1. Sharing your password with friends is a safe online practice.
2. PowerPoint animations can add movement to text and images on slides.

Choose the correct answer from the given options. **(1 X 3 = 3 marks)**

1. Which of the following is not recommended for online safety?
a) Keeping personal information private
b) Using strong passwords
c) Sharing your location publicly
d) Reporting suspicious messages
2. What type of PowerPoint animation effect makes an object leave the slide?
a) Entrance
b) Emphasis
c) Exit
d) Motion Path
3. What is PowerPoint used for?
a) Office presentation
b) Market place
c) At home
d) All of the above

Short answer types of questions. **(1 X 5 = 5 marks)**

1. What is the purpose of using animations in PowerPoint?
2. Name one type of PowerPoint animation effect.
3. Why should personal information not be shared online?
4. What does a strong password include?
5. What is the purpose of privacy settings on social media?

Chapter 5: Email and Internet

In this chapter you will learn about:

Understand the Internet and its various uses.
Explain the purpose and benefits of email.
Create and use an email account.
Sign in and manage an email account.
Compose and send emails effectively.
View, reply, and forward emails.
Sign out securely from email accounts.
Recognize other Internet communication services and their uses.

Internet

What is the Internet?

The Internet is a massive network that connects computers, tablets, phones, and other devices all around the world. Imagine a giant web that links millions of devices, allowing them to share information and communicate with each other. The Internet makes it possible for us to do things like learn new facts, watch videos, play games, and even chat with friends who might live far away.

How does the Internet work?

When you use the Internet, your device (like a computer or smartphone) connects to other devices through a network. Think of it like sending a letter—but instead of waiting days or weeks, messages travel in seconds! Websites, games, videos, and messages are all stored on special computers called "servers." The Internet helps deliver this information quickly to your device when you want to access it.

Uses of the Internet: The Internet is full of interesting things to explore and learn about. Here are some of the main ways people use it:

Learning and Research:
You can find answers to questions, read articles, watch educational videos, and even take online classes.
Websites like Wikipedia or Google make it easy to look up information on almost any topic.
Communication:
The Internet helps us stay in touch with people, even if they are on the other side of the world.
Email, video calls, and messaging apps allow us to talk and share information instantly.
Entertainment:
The Internet is home to fun things like games, movies, music, and videos.
YouTube and streaming sites offer countless videos and songs you can enjoy.
Shopping and Services:
You can buy things online, like books, clothes, or toys, without needing to go to a store.
Many people also use the Internet to book tickets, order food, or schedule appointments.

Staying safe on the Internet While the Internet is a wonderful tool, it's important to stay safe:
Don't share personal information: Keep details like your address, phone number, or school name private.

Ask for help if you're unsure: If you see something that makes you uncomfortable, ask a parent or teacher for advice.
Use trusted websites: Stick to websites that you know are safe and helpful.

Email

What is Email?
Email, short for electronic mail, is a way to send messages online. Instead of writing on paper and waiting for the mail to be delivered, you can type a message on your computer, tablet, or phone and send it instantly! With email, you can stay in touch with friends, family, and teachers, no matter where they are.

How does Email work?
Each person has an email address, which works like a digital "home address" for messages. When you send an email, it goes straight to the recipient's inbox, which is like a mailbox on their device. They can read it immediately, reply, or even forward it to someone else.

Parts of an Email Address an email address is usually made up of three parts:
Username: The first part of the email address is the person's unique name or ID.
@ Symbol: This symbol separates the username from the email provider.
Email Provider: The last part shows which service is used, like **gmail.com** or **yahoo.com**.

For example, in the address **student123@gmail.com**:
"student123" is the username,
"gmail.com" is the provider.

Why use Email?
Email is helpful for many reasons:
Instant communication: Messages are sent and received quickly, so you don't have to wait long to hear back.

Sharing files: You can attach documents, photos, and videos to an email and send them to someone.
Keeping records: Emails are saved in your inbox so that you can look back at old messages anytime.

Basic terms in Email

Inbox: This is where all new messages appear when you receive them.
Compose: When you write a new message, you are "composing" an email.
Subject: This is a short line at the top of your email that tells the recipient what the email is about.
Attachment: Files, like photos or documents you can email.

How to write an Email

Open your email and click "Compose" or "New Message."
Type the recipient's email address in the "To" field.
Add a subject to let them know what your message is about.
Write your message in the central area.
Click "Send" to deliver your email.

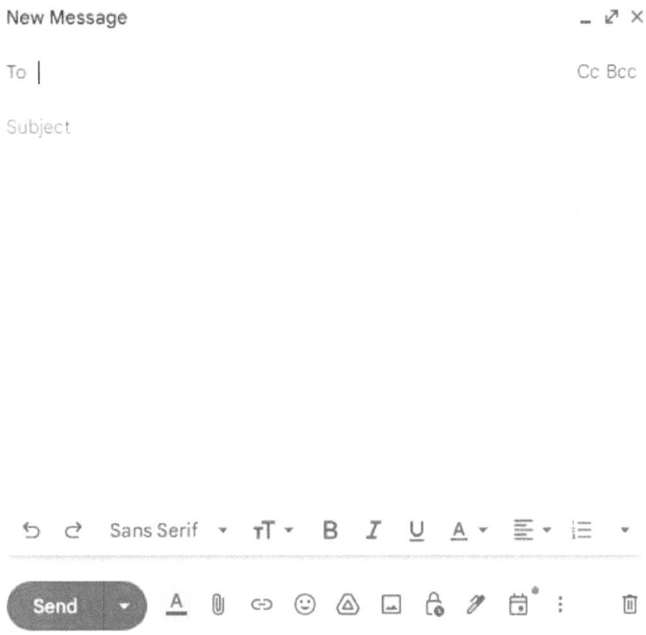

Email Etiquette (Good Habits)

Be Polite: Always start with a greeting, like "Hello" or "Dear."
Be Clear and Concise: Keep your message short and to the point.
Check before sending: Read over your email to make sure there are no spelling mistakes or missing information.

Emails are a simple and effective way to communicate with people quickly. By using email wisely and following good habits, you can stay in touch with others safely and respectfully.

Creating an Email Account

What is an Email Account?

An email account is like a digital mailbox where you can send and receive messages, known as emails. You need to sign up with an email provider, such as Gmail or Yahoo, to have an email account. This account gives you a unique email address, like **student123@gmail.com**, which others can use to reach you.

Why do you need an email account?

An email account helps you:

Stay connected: You can instantly message family, friends, and teachers.

Share files and photos: You can attach documents, pictures, and videos to share.

Sign Up for online activities: Many websites and apps require an email address to sign up for online classes or newsletters.

Steps to create an email account

Choose an Email provider

Some popular email providers include Gmail, Yahoo Mail, and Outlook. Gmail is widely used and is easy to navigate, so we'll use it as an example.

Go to the Email provider's website

Open a web browser (like Chrome or Safari) and type www.gmail.com in the address bar.

Click on create account

You'll see an option on the Gmail homepage that says "Create Account." Click on it to start setting up your email.

Fill in your information

You'll be asked to enter details such as your first and last name and desired email address (username).

Choose a username that's easy for you to remember, such as your name and some numbers, such as **john123@gmail.com.**

Create a strong password

Make sure your password has a mix of letters, numbers, and symbols to keep your account safe. For example, a strong password might look like **St@rFish!21**.

Write down your password somewhere safe so you don't forget it.

Verify your account

You might need to enter a phone number or another email to verify your account. This helps keep your account secure.

Agree to the terms and conditions

Read through the terms of service, then click "Agree" to finish creating your account.

Tips for keeping your email account safe

Do not share your password: Only you should know your password.

Log out on shared devices: If you use a public computer, log out of your email account when you're done.

Use a unique password: Avoid using the same password for other accounts.

Once you complete these steps, your email account is ready! You can start sending and receiving emails and keeping in touch with friends, family, and classmates. Having your email account opens up a world of possibilities for learning and communication!

Signing into a Gmail Account

What Does It Mean to Sign In?
Signing into your Gmail account means entering your email address and password to access your inbox and use all Gmail features. You can view, send, and manage your emails when you sign in.

Why Is Signing In Important?
You need to sign in to access your email account and read or send messages. Signing in ensures that only you (or someone with your permission) can access your emails, keeping your messages private and secure.

Steps to Sign in to Your Gmail Account

Go to the Gmail website
Open a web browser (like Chrome or Firefox), type www.gmail.com in the address bar, and press Enter.
Enter your Email address
You'll see a box that says "Email" or "Enter your email." Type your Gmail address (like student123@gmail.com) and click "Next."
Enter your password
After you enter your email, you'll be prompted to enter your password. Please type your password carefully and make sure it's correct.
Click "Next" again after entering your password.
Access your inbox
You'll be taken to your Gmail inbox once you enter the correct email and password. Here, you can see new messages, reply to emails, and compose new ones.

Tips for Signing In securely
Check for spelling: Double-check that you typed your email and password correctly.
Keep your password private: Never share your password with friends. This will keep your account safe from unauthorized access.
Use "Remember Me" on personal devices: If you're on a personal computer, you can check the "Remember Me" or "Stay Signed In" box to stay signed in. Don't use this option on shared or public devices.
Troubleshooting Sign-In issues
Forgotten password: If you forget your password, click on "Forgot Password" and follow the steps to reset it.
Incorrect email: Make sure you entered the right email address without typos.

Why It's Important to Sign Out When using a shared or public computer, always remember to sign out when you're done to keep your account secure. This way, no one else can access your messages.

Sending an Email

What does it mean to send an email?

Sending an email means composing a message on your email account and delivering it to someone else's email address. You can use email to send information, ask questions, and even share photos or files with others.

Why send Emails?

Emails are a fast and convenient way to communicate with people, whether they're near or far. You can use email to:

Send messages to friends, family, or teachers.

Share files like photos, homework, or documents.

Get quick responses without having to meet in person.

Steps to Send an Email Using Gmail

Open your Gmail Account

First, sign in to your Gmail account by going to www.gmail.com and entering your email address and password.

Click on "Compose"

Once you're in your inbox, look for the "Compose" button, usually on the left side of the screen. Click on it to start writing a new email.

Enter the Recipient's Email Address

In the "To" field, type the email address of the person you want to send the message to. Ensure there are no typos, as the email will only reach the correct address.

Add a Subject

The "Subject" is a short line that tells the recipient what your email is about. For example, if you ask about homework, you might write "Math Homework Question."

Write your Message

In the main body area, type your message. You can start with a greeting like "Hello" or "Dear" and be polite in your message.

Keep the message clear and to the point.

Attach Files (Optional)

If you want to send a file, like a photo or a document, click the paperclip icon (usually at the bottom of the Compose window). Select the file you want to attach from your computer.

Click "Send"

Once your email is ready, click the "Send" button to deliver it to the recipient.

Email Tips for Clear Communication

Be polite: Start with a greeting and end with a closing, like "Thank you" or "Best regards."

Double-check for mistakes: Read your message and check for spelling or grammar errors.

Add a clear subject line: A good subject line helps the recipient understand your email at a glance.

What Happens After You Send the Email?

Once you click "Send," your email is delivered almost instantly to the recipient's inbox. They can open it, read your message, and reply if needed.
Sending an email is simple, and it's a great way to communicate effectively. By following these steps, you can confidently send emails to connect with others!

Viewing an Email

What does it mean to view an email?
Viewing an email means opening and reading a message someone sent you. When you receive an email, it arrives in your **inbox**, where all your new messages are stored.

Why view emails?
Checking and viewing your emails allows you to:
Stay updated on essential messages from friends, family, teachers, or other contacts.
Respond quickly to requests or questions.
Keep track of any attachments that someone may have sent you, like documents or photos.

Steps to view an email in Gmail

Sign into your Gmail account.
Go to www.gmail.com and sign in by entering your email address and password.
Go to your inbox
After signing in, you will automatically be taken to your inbox, where you can see all your received emails.
Find unread emails
Unread emails are usually in bold font to help spot new messages easily.
Look through the list of emails to find any new or unread messages.
Click on an email to open it
Click on the email you want to view. This will open the message, allowing you to read its contents.
Read the message
Once you open the email, read the message carefully. The email may contain text, images, links, or attachments.
View any attachments (If Available)
If the sender has included attachments (like photos or documents), you'll see them at the bottom of the email. Click on the attachment to open or download it.

Tips for organising and managing Emails
Mark as unread: If you need to return to an email later, mark it as "unread" to remind yourself.
Use labels or folders: Gmail allows you to organise emails by adding labels or moving them into folders. For example, you can create a "School" folder for all school-related messages.
Archive Emails: If you don't need an email but want to keep it, you can archive it to keep your inbox clean.

Why it's important to check emails regularly: Regularly checking your email helps you stay on top of important messages and respond promptly. This is especially helpful if you're expecting a reply or waiting for an important update.

Viewing an email is simple, and with these steps, you can stay organised and keep track of all your messages in Gmail!

Replying and Forwarding Emails

What does it mean to Reply and Forward Emails?

Replying to an email means responding directly to the person who sent it. This is useful when you want to answer questions or continue a conversation.

Forwarding an email means sending the same message to someone else. You might do this to share information with another person or to involve them in the conversation.

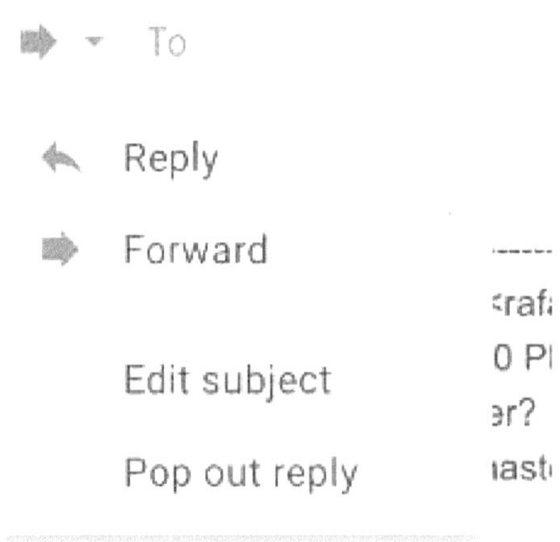

Why Reply and Forward Emails?

Replying lets you keep a conversation and respond quickly to someone's message.

Forwarding helps you share critical information or attachments with others without retreating the message.

Steps to reply to an Email in Gmail

Open the Email

Sign in to your Gmail account, go to your inbox, and click on the email you want to reply to.

Click on "Reply"

Look for the "Reply" button, usually at the bottom of the email. Click on it to open a reply box below the original message.

Type your response

In the reply box, write your message. You can refer to the original email to make sure you answer any questions or address any points made.

Click "Send"

When you've finished writing your reply, click "Send" to deliver it back to the person who sent the original email.

Steps to Forward an Email in Gmail

Open the Email

Sign in to your Gmail account and click on the email you want to forward.

Click on "Forward"

Look for the "Forward" button, usually near the "Reply" button or at the bottom of the email. Click on it to start forwarding the message.

Enter the Recipient's Email Address
In the "To" field, type the email address of the person you want to forward the email to.
Add a Message (Optional)
You can add a short note above the forwarded message to explain what you are sharing.
Click "Send"
Once everything is ready, click "Send" to forward the email to the new recipient.

Tips for Replying and Forwarding Emails
Be clear and polite: Keep your message polite and straightforward when replying.
Check before forwarding: If you forward an email to someone else, ensure the original sender's information can be shared.
Use "Reply All" carefully: If the email was sent to multiple people, "Reply All" will send your reply to everyone in the original email. Use this only if your response is relevant to everyone.

Replying and forwarding are essential email features that make communication easy. They allow you to answer messages quickly and share important information with others!

Signing Out of a Gmail Account

What Does It Mean to Sign Out?
Signing out of your Gmail account means logging out to ensure no one else can access your emails after you've finished using them. This is especially important when using a shared or public computer, like one in a library or school.

Why is Signing Out necessary?
Protects your privacy: When you sign out, it ensures that no one else can view your emails, personal information, or files.
Prevents unauthorised access: Signing out prevents others from accidentally or intentionally accessing your account and sending emails in your name.

Steps to Sign Out of your Gmail account
Locate your profile icon
After you've finished using Gmail, look for your profile icon in the top right corner of the screen. It's usually a circle with your picture or the first letter of your name.
Click on the profile icon
Click on your profile icon to open a dropdown menu.
Select "Sign Out"
You'll see an option in the dropdown menu that says "Sign Out." Click on it to log out of your Gmail account.
Confirm Sign Out (If Needed)
Sometimes, Gmail may ask you to confirm that you want to sign out, especially if you're signed in on multiple devices. Confirm if prompted.

Tips for staying secure on shared devices
Always Sign Out: If you're using a computer that others have access to, like in a school or library, always remember to sign out when you're finished.
Avoid "Remember Me" on public computers: When signing in on a shared device, avoid using the "Remember Me" or "Stay Signed In" options, which can keep you signed in after closing the browser.
Double-Check: After signing out, you can close the browser to ensure your account is completely logged out.

Signing out of your Gmail account is a simple but essential step to protect your privacy and keep your information safe. By following these steps, you can ensure that your account remains secure!

Other Communication Services on the Internet

What Are Communication Services on the Internet?

Apart from email, there are many other ways to communicate over the Internet. These services allow us to connect instantly with people through messages, voice, or video, making staying in touch with friends, family, and even classmates or teachers easy.

Popular Internet Communication Services

Instant Messaging

- Instant messaging apps, like **WhatsApp, Facebook Messenger**, and **iMessage**, let you send and receive text messages instantly.
- You can also share images, videos, voice messages, and documents.
- Many apps allow group chats, where multiple people can talk together in one conversation.

Video Calls

- Video calling apps, such as **Zoom, Skype, and Google Meet**, let you have face-to-face conversations over the Internet, even if the other person is far away.
- Video calls are helpful for online classes, family meetings, or talking to friends.
- Some apps allow multiple people to join, making hosting group meetings or virtual gatherings easy.

Voice Calls Over the Internet

- Services like **WhatsApp and Skype** allow voice-only calls over the Internet.
- This is like a phone call, but it uses the Internet instead of phone lines, which can be cheaper or even accessible.

Social Media

- Social media platforms like **Facebook, Instagram**, and **Twitter** let you connect with others, share updates, photos, and videos, and follow what's happening worldwide.
- You can interact by liking, commenting, and sharing posts, which helps you stay connected with friends and family.

Forums and Discussion Boards

- Forums and discussion boards are online spaces where people with similar interests can share ideas, ask questions, and discuss topics.
- Websites like **Reddit** and hobby-specific forums allow people to join communities based on shared interests, such as sports, games, or books.

Benefits of using communication services

Instant connectivity: These services allow you to communicate instantly, no matter where the other person is.

Multiple ways to connect: Depending on your preference and situation, you can choose to communicate by text, voice, or video.

Access to communities: Many services allow you to join groups or communities, making meeting people with similar interests easy.

Staying safe while using communication services

Use privacy settings: Many apps allow you to control who can see your posts or contact you.
Don't share personal information: Avoid sharing personal details like your address or phone number with strangers.
Be Respectful and Kind: Treat others online the same way you would in person.

These communication services make it easy and fun to stay connected with people around the world, giving us a variety of ways to talk, share, and interact online.

Summary

The Internet connects devices worldwide, enabling learning, communication, entertainment, and online services.
Email, or electronic mail, allows instant communication and is widely used to share messages and files.
Creating an email account is simple, providing a unique address for sending and receiving messages.
Signing in to an email account allows access to view, send, and manage emails, while signing out protects privacy.
Sending an email involves composing a message, adding a recipient, and sending it securely.
Viewing, replying, and forwarding emails enable effective and organized communication.
Other internet communication services include instant messaging, video calls, voice calls, social media, and forums.

Glossary

Internet: A global network that connects computers and devices, allowing information sharing and communication.
Email: A digital method of sending messages instantly over the Internet.
Inbox: The primary folder in an email account where received messages are stored.
Compose: To create and write a new email message.
Subject: A short title or summary of an email's content.
Attachment: A file, such as a photo or document, included with an email.
Username: The first part of an email address, unique to each user.
Instant Messaging: Apps that enable real-time text conversations over the Internet.
Video Calls: Face-to-face communication over the Internet using video.
Social Media: Online platforms where users connect, share, and communicate.
Privacy Settings: Controls that help users manage who can see their information online.
Sign Out: Logging out of an account to protect privacy on shared or public devices.

Exercise

Exercise 1 – Choose the correct answer from the given options.

1. What does the Internet allow us to do?
a) Connect devices worldwide
b) Only play games
c) Only communicate with friends
d) Only shop online

2. Which of these is NOT a part of an email address?
a) Username
b) Subject
c) @ Symbol
d) Email provider

Exercise 2 – Check if the sentence is true or false.
1. Email allows us to send messages instantly over the Internet.
2. The Internet is only used for playing games and watching videos.

Exercise 3- Fill the blank space with the correct word.
1. The main folder where received emails are stored is called the _______.
2. The "Compose" button in an email account is used to write a _______ email.

Exercise 4- Answer the following question in one word.
1. What do you call the unique address used to send and receive emails?
2. What is a short summary line in an email called?

Exercise 5- Short answer types of question.
1. Name two popular email providers.
2. Why is it important to sign out of your email on a public device?
3. Give one example of an instant messaging app.

Answer

Exercise 1- 1. a) 2. b)
Exercise 2- 1. True 2. False
Exercise 3- 1. Animation 2. Safety
Exercise 4- 1. a) 2. a)

Project

Project Title: Creating a Poster on Email Etiquette and Internet Safety
Objective:
To reinforce the rules of email etiquette and internet safety through a creative activity.
Instructions:
Research good email practices and internet safety rules.
Design a colourful poster that includes:
Three important rules for email etiquette (like using clear subjects, being polite, and checking for errors).
Three tips for staying safe online (like not sharing personal info and using strong passwords).
Share the poster with classmates or display it in your classroom to help everyone remember these important rules.

Activity

Title: Email and Internet Safety Quiz Game

To reinforce students' understanding of email etiquette and internet safety principles through a quick, interactive quiz game that encourages teamwork and recall of key safety concepts.

Case Study

Internet Safety and Email Etiquette

Scenario:

Ananya Class 5 student, Ananya recently created her first email account with her parents' help. She is excited to communicate with her friends and family using email. One day, she receives an email from an unknown sender with the subject line "Congratulations! You've won a prize!" The email asks her to click a link and provide her details to claim the prize. Ananya isn't sure what to do, so she asks you for advice.

Questions:

What advice would you give Ananya about handling emails from unknown senders?
Why is it important not to share personal information with strangers online?
How can Ananya identify trustworthy emails?

Group Discussion

The Importance of Online Communication and Safety

Objective:

To help students understand the various ways to communicate safely over the internet and the importance of protecting personal information.

Online Interactive Resources

Online Exam Paper

Link: https://forms.gle/6W1Wui6FosLAKDp98

QR Code:

Chapter 5 Videos

Link: https://www.youtube.com/playlist?list=PLzlh_31VWEFp9BLDUWpukbGGPelJm2Us1

QR Code:

Chapter-5
Test Paper
Internet and Email!

Time Duration: 20 Minutes **Maximum Marks: 10**

General Instructions:
1. The question paper consists of 10 questions.
2. All questions are compulsory.

SECTION-A

Check if the sentence is true or false. **(1 X 2 = 2 marks)**
1. Signing out of your email account on a shared device helps protect your privacy.
2. Social media platforms are only used for making phone calls.

Choose the correct answer from the given options. **(1 X 3 = 3 marks)**
1. What is the purpose of the "Subject" line in an email?
a) To add a greeting
b) To summarise the email's content
c) To list attachments
d) To write the email's closing
2. Which action is necessary after finishing an email session on a shared computer?
a) Compose a new email
b) Sign out of your email account
c) Delete the inbox
d) Change the password
3. Which of these is a video-calling app?
a) WhatsApp
b) Zoom
c) Twitter
d) Google Search

Short answer types of questions. **(1 X 5 = 5 marks)**
1. What is the purpose of the "Attachment" option in an email?
2. Name two uses of the Internet.
3. What does "Reply All" do in an email?
4. Why should you avoid sharing personal information on public websites?
5. What is one benefit of using video calling apps?

Chapter 6: Let's Play with Computers and Coding

In this chapter you will learn about:

Understanding the concept of an Algorithm and its applications.
Recognizing the purpose and types of Loops in programming.
Identifying Input and Output processes and their significance in coding.
Developing Problem-Solving skills in programming.
Creating Mini-Programs to apply coding concepts practically.

What's an Algorithm?

What is an Algorithm?
An Algorithm is a set of step-by-step instructions for solving a problem or completing a task. Think of it like following a recipe when you're cooking: each step guides you toward the end result, and if you follow all the steps in the right order, you'll get the outcome you want. In computing, algorithms help computers know exactly what to do.

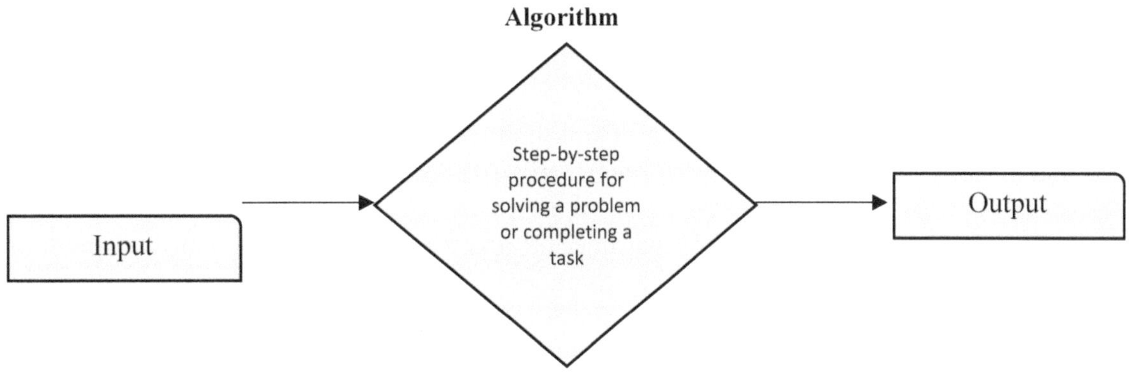

Simple example of an Algorithm: Imagine making a peanut butter and jelly sandwich. Here's a basic algorithm for it:
Take two slices of bread.
Spread peanut butter on one slice.
Spread jelly on the other slice.
Put the slices together.
Enjoy your sandwich!

If you follow each step correctly, you'll end up with a sandwich. This is just like how computers follow algorithms to complete tasks.

Algorithms in everyday life: Algorithms aren't just used by computers; we follow them in our daily lives too:
Getting ready for school: Wake up, brush your teeth, eat breakfast, and get dressed. Each step has to be followed to be ready for school.
Solving math problems: Follow specific steps to add, subtract, multiply, or divide numbers.

Why Are Algorithms important in Computing?
Computers don't understand things the way we do—they need very clear instructions. An algorithm gives the computer a list of tasks in a specific order so it can complete the work quickly and accurately. Without an algorithm, the computer wouldn't know what actions to take.

How Algorithms help us code: In coding, we use algorithms to tell the computer exactly what to do. For example, if we're creating a game, an algorithm might make a character move left or right when the player presses a key.

Activity: Writing your Algorithm
Try writing an algorithm for brushing your teeth. Think about each step you take, starting with picking up your toothbrush. This helps you understand how precise algorithms need to be!

Key takeaway: An algorithm is simply a set of instructions, and it's the foundation of all computer programs. By learning to create algorithms, you're learning to think like a programmer!

Fun with Loops!

What is a Loop?
A Loop is a programming concept that lets you repeat a set of instructions multiple times without having to write them repeatedly. It's like setting up a chore list and asking the computer to "keep doing this until I tell you to stop!" Loops save time and simplify coding, especially when you want to repeat tasks.

Why do we use Loops? Loops help make programs shorter, easier to read, and more efficient. For example, if you want a character in a game to keep moving forward until they reach a certain point, you can use a loop instead of writing "move forward" repeatedly. Loops are instrumental in animations, games, and repetitive tasks.

Types of Loops

For Loop:

A "for" loop repeats an action a specific number of times.
Example: Counting from 1 to 10, where each number is displayed one after the other.
In programming, this might look like:

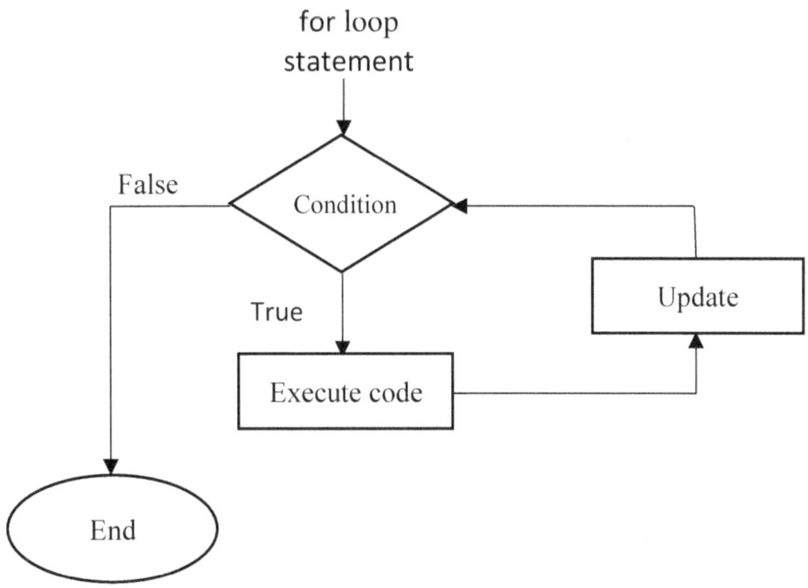

Code:
For each number from 1 to 10:
   Print the number

While Loop:
A "while" loop repeats as long as a condition is true.
Example: Keep adding blocks to a tower until it's ten blocks high.
In programming, it would look something like:

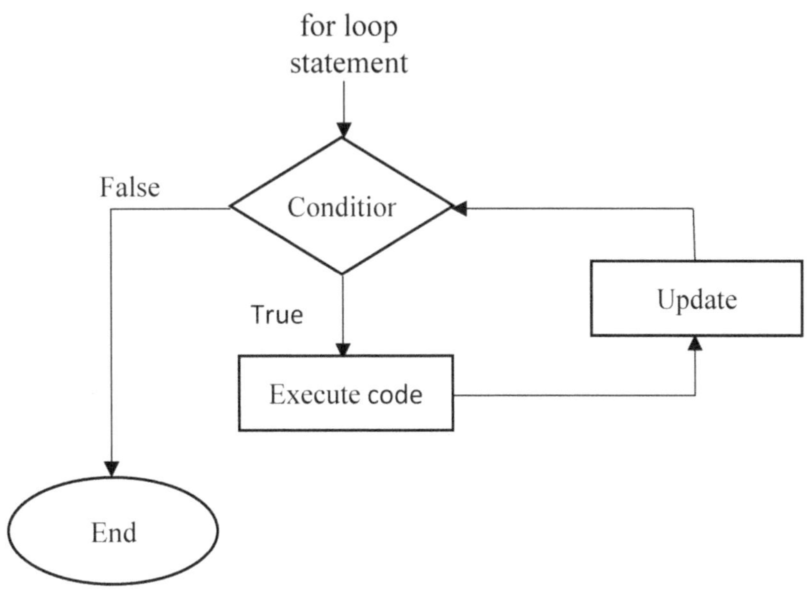

Code:
While the tower has less than 10 blocks:
   Add one block to the tower

Examples of Loops in real life
Washing hands: Imagine you have a loop for washing your hands. You might repeat "scrub for 10 seconds" until a timer reaches twenty seconds.
Exercise routine: Do ten jumping jacks every morning. Instead of writing each "jump" down, you can set a loop to count up to ten.

Activity: Counting with a Loop Try using a loop to count by two up to ten. Write it like this:
Start at two.
Add two each time.
Stop when you reach ten.
This helps you understand how loops save time by reducing the need for repeated steps.

Why are Loops important in Coding?
Loops make coding faster and easier, especially for repetitive tasks. They allow the computer to complete a task many times without writing the same code repeatedly. Loops are essential for creating games, animations, and even simple calculators.

Key takeaway: Loops let us repeat actions quickly and efficiently, saving time and improving our programs. By learning to use loops, you can make your programs and games run faster and more smoothly!

Input and Output: Talk to your computer

What is Input? Input is any information or data you give the computer to help it understand what you want it to do. Inputs are like questions or instructions that you "ask" the computer, and they can come from typing on a keyboard, clicking a mouse, touching a screen, or even speaking into a microphone.

Examples of Input:
Typing a search: When you type "What's the weather today?" into a search engine, that's input.
Pressing buttons in a game: Each time you press a button, you give input to control the character.
Giving voice commands: Saying "Play music" to a smart device is also an input.

What is Output?
Output is how the computer responds to the input you've given. It's the computer's way of "talking back" to you or showing the results. Outputs can appear as text on a screen, sounds, images, or even printed pages.

Examples of Output:

Display on screen: Seeing search results after you type a query.
Game sounds and visuals: Hearing sound effects or seeing your character move in response to your controls.
Printed documents: A printer creates an output by printing your requested document.

How Input and Output work together Input and output are like a conversation between you and the computer:
You give an Input: You type a question or press a button.
The Computer processes it: The computer thinks about what you've asked or done.
The Computer gives an Output: It shows you the answer on the screen or acts.

For example:
In a calculator app: You input numbers and operations, like 5 + 3. The calculator processes the input and outputs the answer, which is 8.

Why Are Input and Output important in coding? When programming, input and output help us create interactive programs that respond to the user's actions. They make programs more engaging, allowing users to type in commands, make choices, or see results.

Activity: Make your Input-Output system.
Try setting up a simple input-output exercise on paper:
Write a "question" (input), like "What 5 + 3 is?"
Write an "answer" (output), like "The answer is 8."
This will help you see how inputs and outputs work together to create interaction.

Key Takeaway: Input is how you give instructions to the computer, and output is how the computer responds. Together, they enable interaction with programs, search for information, and control games or devices.

Solve problems like a pro!

What is Problem Solving?
Problem-solving is the process of finding a solution to a challenge or question. In programming, it means figuring out a way to make the computer do what you want it to do. Problem-solving is essential in coding because it helps break down complex tasks into simple, manageable steps.

Steps to Problem Solving

Understand the problem
Carefully read or think about what needs to be solved.
Example: If you're creating a game, you need to understand what the player should be able to do, like move a character or score points.
Plan a Solution
Think about the steps or algorithms needed to solve the problem.

Write down the steps in a sequence that will lead to the solution.
Example: If you're making a program to add two numbers, the plan could be: "Take the first number, take the second number, add them, and show the result."

Write the Solution (Code It)

Use the plan to write code, making sure each step is followed.
Example: In a calculator app, write code that takes two inputs (numbers), performs the addition, and outputs the result.

Test and Fix

Run the code to see if it works correctly. If it doesn't, find the problem and fix it.
Testing helps ensure the solution works as expected and identifies any "bugs" (mistakes) in the code.

Example of Problem-Solving: Creating a Maze Game

Suppose you want to create a simple maze game where a player has to reach the exit without hitting any walls. Here's how you'd apply the problem-solving steps:

Understand: What should happen? The player should be able to move through the maze and reach the end without hitting walls.

Plan: Decide on the steps to make this work, like setting up walls, creating a player character, and adding movement controls.

Code: Write the code for each part—create the maze, make the character move, and detect collisions with walls.

Test: Play the game to make sure everything works. If the player moves through walls, fix the code to prevent that.

Why Problem-Solving is Important in Coding Problem-solving skills help coders approach any task with confidence. Whether you're creating a game, app, or website, using a step-by-step approach makes it easier to turn ideas into reality.

Activity: Solve a simple problem using steps

Choose a small problem, like creating a to-do list on paper:
Understand: You want to list tasks for the day.
Plan: Write down each task in order.
Write (Do): List the tasks.
Test: Check if you have all tasks written down and add any missing ones.

Key takeaway: Problem-solving helps break down tasks into clear steps. By understanding, planning, coding, and testing, you can solve almost any problem in programming and bring your ideas to life!

Make Your Mini-Programs

What is a Mini Program?

A mini program is a small, simple program that performs a specific task, such as a calculator, a guessing game, or a countdown timer. Making mini-programs is a fun way to practice coding and bring your ideas to life!

Why make Mini Programs?

Creating mini-programs helps you understand how to code and combine different concepts like algorithms, loops, input/output, and problem-solving. Mini programs are great for experimenting and learning coding skills step-by-step.

Steps to make a Mini Program

Choose an Idea

Think of a small task you want the computer to do. Examples: a program that adds two numbers, a game that guesses a number, or a quiz.

Could you keep it simple to start?

Plan the Algorithm

Write down the steps (algorithm) your program will follow. For example, in a guessing game:

Ask the player to guess a number.

Compare the guess with the correct answer.

Tell the player if they are correct or need to try again.

Code with Loops and Input/Output

Use code to put your algorithm into action. Include loops if you want to repeat steps (like asking the player to guess again) and use input/output to make the program interactive.

Example: If making a countdown, use a loop to count down from 10 to 1, displaying each number.

Test Your Program

Run your program to see if it works as expected. If there are issues, find and fix them. This process is called "debugging."

For example, if the program doesn't end correctly, check your loop or conditions to see what needs fixing.

Examples of Mini Programs you can try

Simple calculator: A program that inputs two numbers and outputs the sum, difference, or product.

Guess the number game: A game where the player tries to guess a randomly chosen number.

Mini quiz: Ask questions, then calculate and display the score.

Activity: Create your first mini-program

Choose a simple idea (e.g., a program that says "Hello!" a certain number of times).

Plan the steps (e.g., get input for the number of times, then use a loop to print "Hello!").

Write and test the code.

Key takeaway: Making mini-programs lets you practice coding, be creative, and solve problems in a fun way. Each mini-program is a chance to learn something new and see how coding can turn ideas into interactive, valuable tools.

Summary

A set of ordered steps to solve a problem or complete a task, similar to following a recipe.

Loops: Instructions that repeat a task multiple times, like "for" and "while" loops.

Input/Output: Input is data given to a computer, and output is the computer's response.

Problem-Solving: Breaking down tasks into steps to find solutions.

Mini-Programs: Small, focused programs for specific tasks, helping to apply coding skills

Glossary

Algorithm: Step-by-step instructions for solving a problem.
Loop: A programming construct that repeats a set of instructions.
For Loop: Repeats an action a specified number of times.
While Loop: Repeats as long as a condition is true.
Input: Data or instructions provided to the computer.
Output: The result or response from the computer.
Problem-Solving: A process to find solutions through defined steps.
Mini-Program: A small program created for a specific task.
Debugging: The process of finding and fixing errors in code.

Exercise

Exercise 1 – Choose the correct answer from the given options.

1. What is an algorithm?
a) A type of loop in programming
b) A set of step-by-step instructions to solve a problem
c) The result of a computer process
d) A storage device in a computer
2. Which type of loop repeats as long as a condition is true?
a) For loop
b) While loop
c) Do loop
d) Forever loop

Exercise 2 – Check if the sentence is true or false.

1. Loops are used to repeat tasks in programming to make code more efficient.
2. An algorithm is only used in computer programming, not in daily life.

Exercise 3- Fill the blank space with the correct word.

1. Input is the information given to a computer, while _______ is the response or result from the computer.
2. A mini-program is a small program created to perform a _______ task.

Exercise 4- Choose the odd one out.

1. Algorithm, Loop, Monitor, Problem-Solving
2. For loop, While loop, Do loop, Output

Exercise 5- Short answer types of question.

1. What is the purpose of a loop in programming?
2. How does input and output create interaction with a program?
3. Why are algorithms important in computing?

Answer

Exercise 1- 1. b) 2. b)
Exercise 2- 1. True 2. False
Exercise 3- 1. Output 2. Specific
Exercise 4- 1. Monitor 2. Output

Project

Project Title: Design an Interactive Quiz Program
Objective: Create a simple interactive quiz program to practice using input, output, and loops in programming.
Instructions:

Design a quiz with 5 questions on a topic of your choice.
Write an algorithm for the quiz program, specifying how you'll use input (for question display and user answers) and output (for showing correct/incorrect responses).
Use a loop to display each question and keep track of the score.
Display the final score at the end of the quiz.

Activity

Create an Algorithm for a Treasure Hunt
Objective: Write an algorithm to guide a friend to a "hidden treasure" in the classroom or playground.
Instructions:

Hide a small object (like a toy or note) somewhere in the room or playground.
Write a detailed algorithm with step-by-step instructions to help a friend locate the treasure. Include directions like "take three steps forward" or "turn left."
Test your algorithm by swapping with a partner and following each other's instructions.

Task: Create a clear, precise algorithm for finding the hidden treasure, and exchange it with a friend to see if they can follow it accurately.

Case Study

A Student's Daily Routine Algorithm
Scenario: Riya, a student, must create an algorithm for her daily morning routine to ensure she's on time for school. Her routine includes waking up, brushing her teeth, eating breakfast, and getting dressed.
Questions to Consider:

What step-by-step tasks should Riya include in her algorithm?
How can she use loops to repeat daily parts of her routine?
How would you ensure each step in the algorithm is straightforward and easy to follow?

Task: Develop an algorithm for Riya's morning routine, organising each step logically. Consider using loops or conditional steps to make the routine efficient.

Group Discussion

The Importance of Input and Output in Everyday Devices
Topic: Discuss how input and output functions work in devices you use daily, such as smartphones, gaming consoles, and computers.

Online Interactive Resources

Online Exam Paper
Link: https://forms.gle/2dffiQ1KBnnHVFnp8
QR Code:

Chapter 6 Videos
Link: https://www.youtube.com/playlist?list=PLzlh_31VWEFqNtkb7PUObyjnQ9I775SwD
QR Code:

Chapter-6
Test Paper
Let's Play with Computers and Coding

Time Duration: 20 Minutes **Maximum Marks: 10**

General Instructions:
1. The question paper consists of 10 questions.
2. All questions are compulsory.

SECTION-A

Check if the sentence is true or false. **(1 X 2 = 2 marks)**
1. Loops are used to repeat tasks in programming.
2. Input is the data given by the user to the computer.

Choose the correct answer from the given options. **(1 X 3 = 3 marks)**
1. What is an algorithm?
a) Storage device
b) Set of instructions
c) Screen control
d) Hardware
2. Which loop repeats a specific number of times?
a) While loop
b) For loop
c) Until loop
d) If loop
3. In programming, input is:
a) Instructions for the computer
b) Result on the screen
c) Data storage
d) Display action

Short answer types of questions. **(1 X 5 = 5 marks)**
1.What is an algorithm?
2.Why are loops useful?
3.Give an example of input.
4.What is the purpose of output?
5.Name a type of loop.

Chapter 7: Robotics

In this chapter you will learn about:

- Understanding the meaning and importance of Robotics.
- Exploring the impact of robots on jobs and the workforce.
- Differentiating between automatic machines and robots.
- Recognizing the relationship between Artificial Intelligence (AI) and Robotics.
- Identifying examples of robots in various fields.

Meaning of Robotics

What is Robotics?

Robotics is the field of science and technology focused on designing, building, and using robots. A **robot** is a machine created to perform tasks, sometimes even without human guidance. These tasks can range from simple activities, like moving objects, to more complex jobs, such as assisting in surgeries or exploring outer space. Robotics combines knowledge from different areas, including engineering, computer science, and electronics, to create machines that can move, sense, and respond to their environment.

Understanding Robots:

A robot is much more than a regular machine. Unlike basic machines that only perform a single task, robots are often programmable and can adapt to various situations. For example, some robots can sense obstacles and change direction, while others can recognize objects or even understand voice commands.

Examples of Robots in everyday life:

- **Robot vacuums**: Small robots that automatically clean floors by moving around and avoiding obstacles.
- **Robotic arms in factories**: These robots help assemble products like cars or electronics with great accuracy and speed.
- **Drones**: Flying robots that can take pictures, deliver packages, and explore areas that may be difficult for humans to reach.

Why is Robotics important? Robots help people complete tasks more efficiently, safely, and accurately. Here's why robotics is essential:

- **Efficiency**: Robots can work without breaks, which means they can complete tasks faster.
- **Safety**: Robots can perform dangerous tasks, like working in extreme conditions, which keeps people safe.
- **Precision**: Robots can perform tasks with incredible accuracy, which is essential in areas like medicine and manufacturing.

Fields that use Robots: Robots are used in various fields, including:

- **Healthcare**: Assisting doctors in surgeries and patient care.

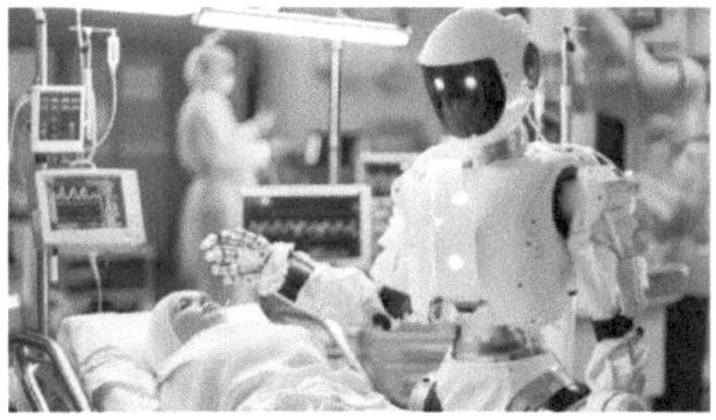

Manufacturing: Assembling products in factories quickly and accurately.

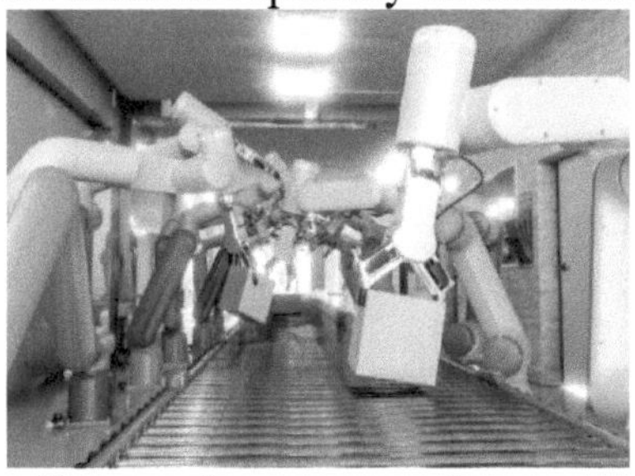

Exploration: Robots are sent to explore distant planets or underwater areas where humans can't go easily.

Fun fact: Some robots are designed to look and act like humans! These are called **humanoid robots** and are often used in research to understand how robots can interact with people in more natural ways.

Key takeaway: Robotics is a fascinating field that combines technology, science, and creativity to build machines that help us in many ways. Robots are becoming a bigger part of our lives, from cleaning our homes to helping scientists explore space!

Threat to Jobs

Can Robots take over Jobs?

As robotics and automation continue to advance, there is a concern that robots might replace certain jobs, especially those involving repetitive or routine tasks. Robots are very efficient at doing the same task repeatedly without getting tired, which makes them useful in industries like manufacturing, customer service, and even some aspects of healthcare. However, while robots might handle some tasks, they also create new job opportunities in fields like robot design, maintenance, and programming.

Examples of Jobs affected by Robots:

Manufacturing jobs: Robots in factories can assemble products quickly and accurately, sometimes replacing tasks previously done by people.

Retail and Customer service: Some stores and hotels use robots to assist customers, answer questions, and handle simple customer service tasks.

Agriculture: Robots are increasingly used for tasks like planting, watering, and harvesting crops.

Will Robots take all jobs?

Not necessarily! Although robots can replace some repetitive tasks, they can't easily do jobs that require creativity, emotional intelligence, or complex decision-making. For instance, jobs like teaching, art, therapy, and management are difficult for robots to replace because they require human interaction and empathy.

New opportunities created by Robots:

With more robots in the workforce, there's also a growing need for people to build, program, and maintain these machines. This means there are more job opportunities in technology, engineering, and computer science. People who work in these fields help design robots, develop software for them, and ensure they run smoothly.

Why humans are still essential:

Humans have qualities that robots lack, such as creativity, problem-solving abilities, and the capacity to understand emotions. Many jobs require these skills, so humans and robots often work together to get the best results. For example, a robot might handle repetitive tasks in a factory, while a human oversees the process and handles any unexpected issues.

How Robots and Humans can work together:

Robots are tools that help humans work more efficiently. For example:

In Hospitals: Robots assist doctors by bringing supplies or even helping with surgeries, but doctors still make the important medical decisions.

In Factories: Robots assemble products, while humans supervise, inspect, and control quality.

Key takeaway: While robots can take over some jobs, they also create new opportunities and help make work safer and more efficient. Robots and humans each have unique strengths, and by working together, they can achieve even more than they could alone.

Automatic Machines and Robots

What Are Automatic Machines? Automatic machines are devices that perform specific tasks without needing much human assistance. They operate based on programmed instructions and follow a set of rules to complete a job. For example, a washing machine automatically runs through different cycles—washing, rinsing, and spinning—based on the settings you choose.

Examples of Automatic Machines:

Washing Machines: You set the wash cycle, and the machine automatically goes through the steps to wash clothes.

Elevators: After pressing a button, the elevator moves to the desired floor without further guidance.

Vending Machines: You insert money, select an item, and the machine dispenses it automatically.

What are Robots? Robots are a special type of automatic machine, but they are often more complex. Unlike basic automatic machines, robots can sense their surroundings, make decisions, and adapt to different situations. Robots are usually programmable and can perform a range of tasks, sometimes even learning as they go.

Difference Between Automatic Machines and Robots:

Automatic Machines: These follow specific, unchanging instructions and don't adapt to new situations. They do one job in a consistent way.

Robots: Robots are usually equipped with sensors and artificial intelligence, allowing them to sense their environment, make decisions, and even learn over time. This makes them more flexible and capable of handling different tasks.

Examples of Robots:

Robot vacuums: These robots move around a house, detecting dirt and avoiding obstacles to clean the floors automatically.

Robotic arms in factories: These robots assemble products and can be programmed to handle different tasks, adjusting as needed.

Drones: Flying robots that can navigate areas, take pictures, and deliver packages.

How Robots and Automatic Machines are used together: In many cases, robots and automatic machines work together to complete tasks more efficiently. For example, in a factory:

Robotic arms assemble products, which are then moved automatically by conveyor belts (automatic machines) to the next station.

Sorting Robots identify and sort items, while automatic machines handle the packaging.

Why Robots are more versatile:

Robots are designed to handle more complex tasks and adapt to their environment. They can perform a range of activities and respond to changes, while automatic machines are limited to specific functions.

Key takeaway: Automatic machines and robots both make our lives easier, but robots are generally more advanced and adaptable. Robots can sense, respond, and even learn, while automatic machines simply follow fixed instructions. Together, they help complete various tasks in industries, homes, and beyond!

Relation between Artificial Intelligence and Robotics

What is Artificial Intelligence (AI)? Artificial Intelligence, or AI, is the ability of a computer or machine to mimic human intelligence. AI allows machines to make decisions, recognize patterns, learn from experiences, and solve problems on their own. AI enables machines to become "smarter" over time by analysing data and improving their actions based on past outcomes.

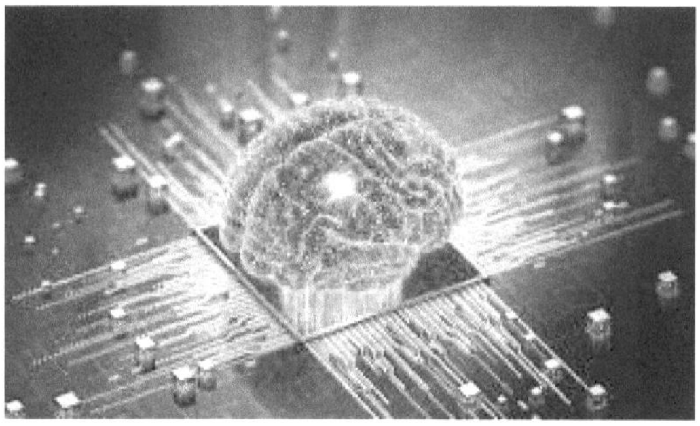

How AI and Robotics work together When AI is combined with robotics, it gives robots the ability to think and make decisions, making them more versatile and capable. With AI, robots can:

- **Recognize objects and people**: AI enables robots to "see" and understand their environment, identifying objects, people, and even facial expressions.
- **Make decisions**: Instead of following strict, fixed instructions, AI-powered robots can choose the best course of action based on their surroundings and objectives.
- **Learn from experience**: AI allows robots to learn from mistakes and improve. For example, a robot with AI can learn to avoid obstacles more effectively over time.

Examples of AI in Robotics:

- **Self-Driving cars**: Self-driving cars use AI to analyse their surroundings, navigate roads, avoid obstacles, and follow traffic rules without human control.
- **Delivery Robots**: Robots that deliver packages can use AI to find the shortest routes, recognize obstacles, and ensure safe delivery.
- **Healthcare Robots**: In hospitals, robots with AI can assist in surgeries, monitor patients, and even make initial diagnoses based on symptoms.

Differences between Robots with and without AI

- **Basic Robots**: These follow a fixed set of instructions and do not learn or adapt. For example, a robotic arm in a factory performs the same task repeatedly without any changes.
- **AI-Powered Robots**: These robots are "intelligent" and can adapt to new situations. They can improve their actions over time, analyse data, and make decisions based on what they learn.

Why AI is important in Robotics

AI makes robots more capable, allowing them to perform complex tasks and adapt to new situations. Robots with AI can be used in areas that require flexibility and problem-solving skills, such as healthcare, customer service, and even space exploration.

How AI and Robotics are shaping the future

The combination of AI and robotics is transforming industries by making machines more efficient and autonomous. With AI, robots can assist in many fields, from helping in classrooms and hospitals to exploring distant planets. This partnership between AI and robotics opens up endless possibilities for what machines can achieve.

Key takeaway: AI brings intelligence to robots, allowing them to think, learn, and adapt. While traditional robots follow set instructions, AI-powered robots can make decisions and respond to changes, making them valuable tools for the future.

Summary

The science of designing and building robots for various tasks, enhancing efficiency, safety, and precision.
Robot vacuums, robotic arms in factories, drones.
Robots can replace repetitive jobs but also create opportunities in tech fields.
Automatic machines follow fixed instructions; robots can sense, adapt, and make decisions.
AI enables robots to recognize objects, make decisions, and learn from experience.
AI-powered robots open new possibilities in fields like healthcare, exploration, and customer service.

Glossary

Robotics: The science and technology of creating robots.
Robot: A programmable machine capable of performing tasks.
Humanoid Robot: A robot designed to resemble and act like a human.
Automation: The use of machines to perform tasks without continuous human input.
Automatic Machine: A machine that performs a task based on fixed instructions.
Artificial Intelligence (AI): Technology that enables machines to mimic human intelligence.
Self-Driving Car: A vehicle that uses AI to operate without a driver.
Drone: A flying robot that can navigate and perform tasks remotely.
Healthcare Robot: A robot used in medical settings to assist with tasks like monitoring or surgeries.
AI-Powered Robot: A robot equipped with AI, allowing it to learn, adapt, and make decisions.

Exercise

Exercise 1 – Choose the correct answer from the given options.

1. What is the primary purpose of robotics?
a) To create machines that perform repetitive tasks only
b) To design machines that can perform tasks, sometimes without human guidance
c) To replace all human jobs with robots
d) To invent automatic household devices
2. Which of these robots is commonly used in healthcare?
a) Robot vacuum

b) Delivery robot
c) Robotic arm for surgeries
d) Drones

Exercise 2 – Check if the sentence is true or false.
1. Automatic machines can adapt to different situations and learn from experience.
2. Artificial Intelligence allows robots to make decisions and learn from experience.

Exercise 3- Fill the blank space with the correct word.
1. A robot vacuum is an example of a robot that can _______ and avoid obstacles.
2. Robots in _______ help in tasks like assisting doctors and performing surgeries.

Exercise 4- Rearrange the sentence.
1. used / drones / areas / explore / difficult / for humans / to reach / are / to
2. of / Robots / efficiency / increase / and / safety

Exercise 5- Short answer types of question.
1.Define robotics in one sentence.
2.Name one job that robots have taken over and explain why.
3.What is the difference between automatic machines and robots?

Answer

Exercise 1- 1. b) 2. c)
Exercise 2- 1. False 2. True
Exercise 3- 1. Sensor 2. Healthcare
Exercise 4- 1. Drones are used to explore areas difficult for humans to reach.
2. Robots increase efficiency and safety.

Project

Project Title: Design a Robot Model
Objective: To understand the components and functionality of a basic robot by creating a model.
Instructions:
Design a model of a simple robot that can perform a task (e.g., a robot vacuum, a robotic arm).
Label the key parts of your robot, such as sensors, "arms," and wheels.
Write a brief description of what task your robot will perform and how it helps people.
Materials: Cardboard, markers, glue, paper, and other household items.

Activity

Activity Title: Plan an "Algorithm" for a Robot Helper
Objective: Write a step-by-step algorithm for a robot helper to complete a task.
Instructions:
Choose a task, like "cleaning a room" or "watering plants."
Write down each step the robot should take, in a sequence it can follow.
Test the algorithm with a friend acting as the "robot" and following your instructions exactly.
Hint: Be clear and specific with each step. A robot will only do exactly what you tell it to.

Case Study

Robots in Healthcare
Scenario: A hospital is using robots to assist with patient care. These robots deliver supplies, help with surgeries, and monitor patients' vital signs. The staff is adapting to these robots, learning to work alongside them for better patient care.
Questions to Consider:
How do these robots improve the efficiency and safety of hospital tasks?
What tasks are still better suited for human doctors and nurses?
How could AI enhance the functionality of these healthcare robots in the future?

Task: Analyse the benefits and limitations of using robots in healthcare and propose ways to improve their integration with AI.

Group Discussion

How Robots are Changing Jobs
Topic: Discuss the impact of robots on jobs and new opportunities created by robotics.
Objective: To understand the role of robots in the workforce and discuss the future balance between human and robotic jobs.

Online Interactive Resources

Online Exam Paper
Link: https://forms.gle/T3zmjjFREpQ2dPit8
QR Code:

Chapter 7 Videos
Link: https://www.youtube.com/playlist?list=PLzlh_31VWEFp8ZeeGUYMIrofZzZm0wyM3
QR Code:

Chapter-7
Test Paper
Robotics

Time Duration: 20 Minutes **Maximum Marks: 10**

General Instructions:
1. The question paper consists of 10 questions.
2. All questions are compulsory.

SECTION-A

Check if the sentence is true or false. **(1 X 2 = 2 marks)**
1. Humanoid robots are designed to look and act like humans.
2. Automatic machines can make decisions and adapt to new situations like robots.

Choose the correct answer from the given options. **(1 X 3 = 3 marks)**
1. Which of the following fields commonly uses robots to assist in surgeries and patient care?
a) Agriculture
b) Healthcare
c) Education
d) Entertainment
2. What is one main difference between automatic machines and robots?
a) Robots can only perform a single task
b) Automatic machines have sensors, while robots do not
c) Robots can sense and adapt to their environment, while automatic machines cannot
d) Automatic machines are used only in homes
3. Which type of robot is used for exploring areas that are difficult for humans to reach?
a) Robot vacuum
b) Robotic arm
c) Drone
d) Humanoid robot

Short answer types of questions. **(1 X 5 = 5 marks)**
1. Define robotics.
2. Give one example of a robot used in everyday life.
3. Why are robots beneficial in manufacturing?
4. What is Artificial Intelligence (AI) in the context of robotics?
5. Name one field where robots are used to explore areas humans cannot easily reach.

Chapter 8: Viva Voce

1.What are the main parts inside a computer?
The main parts inside a computer are the CPU, memory, hard drive, and motherboard.

2.What is the role of the CPU in a computer?
The CPU is known as the "brain" of the computer. It processes instructions and performs calculations.

3.Can you name two input devices and two output devices?
Input devices: Keyboard and mouse. Output devices: Monitor and printer.

4.What is software?
Software is a set of instructions that tells the computer how to perform tasks. It includes operating systems, apps, and programs.

5.What is an example of an application software?
Examples of application software are Microsoft Word, Paint, and games like Minecraft.

6.What does 'adding or removing software' mean?
Adding software means installing new programs, while removing software means uninstalling programs that are no longer needed.

7.What is a table used for in Excel?
In Excel, a table is used to organize and display data in rows and columns, making it easier to read and analyze.

8.How can we link one cell to another in Excel?
We can link one cell to another by entering an equal sign (=) followed by the cell address we want to link.

9.What is PowerPoint used for?
PowerPoint is used to create presentations with slides, text, pictures, and animations.

10.How can we add animations to slides in PowerPoint?
In PowerPoint, we can add animations by selecting text or images on the slide and choosing an animation effect from the "Animations" tab.

11.Why is it important to be safe online?
Being safe online is important to protect our personal information and avoid cyber risks, like viruses or scams.

12.What is the Internet?
The Internet is a global network that connects computers all over the world, allowing us to access websites, send emails, and use online services.

13.What is an email?
An email is a way to send messages, pictures, or files electronically from one computer to another using the Internet.

14.Can you name some steps to create an email account?
To create an email account, go to a website like Gmail, click on "Create account," fill in your information, and follow the instructions.

15.What is an algorithm?
An algorithm is a step-by-step set of instructions to solve a problem or complete a task.

16.What is a loop in coding?
A loop in coding is a sequence of instructions that repeats until a certain condition is met. Loops help save time by automating repetitive tasks.

17.What is robotics?
Robotics is the field that involves designing, building, and operating robots to perform tasks.

18.How are robotics and artificial intelligence connected?
Artificial intelligence (AI) helps robots learn from data, make decisions, and perform tasks more intelligently, making them more useful.

19.What is the purpose of coding?
Coding is used to write instructions for computers, telling them how to perform tasks and create programs or games.

20.Can robots replace human jobs? Why or why not?
Robots can perform some tasks, like repetitive or dangerous jobs, but they cannot replace all human jobs because they lack emotions and creativity.

Online Interactive Resources

Online Exam Paper
Link: https://forms.gle/2S6j6EUBg4Qj3ZjdA

QR Code:

Chapter 8 Videos
Link: https://www.youtube.com/playlist?list=PLzlh_31VWEFr6fOjY9b1U7i2Yq1wKmomV

QR Code:

Annual Test Paper

Time Duration: 40 Minutes **Maximum Marks: 50**

General Instructions:

1. The question paper consists of 45 questions and is divided into four sections, A and B.
2. All questions are compulsory.
3. Section A comprises True/False, Fill in the blanks, One word and Choose the correct option of one mark each.
4. Section B comprises question numbers 1 to 5. These are short questions that carry two marks each.

SECTION-A

Fill in the blanks- **(1 X 10 = 10 marks)**

1. The main storage device of a computer is called the ______.
2. The CPU is known as the ______ of the computer.
3. A device used to display visual information is called a ______.
4. The Internet is a global network that connects ______ around the world.
5. To create a new slide in PowerPoint, you click on ______.
6. In Excel, a ______ is a collection of rows and columns.
7. A ______ is a step-by-step set of instructions used to solve a problem.
8. In an email, the section where we write the recipient's address is called the ______.
9. The function used to add numbers in Excel is called ______.
10. The software that manages a computer's hardware and applications is the ______.

True/False – **(1 X 10 = 10 marks)**

1. The keyboard is an output device. (True/False)
2. PowerPoint is used to create presentations. (True/False)
3. A printer is an input device. (True/False)
4. Loops in coding are used to repeat instructions. (True/False)
5. Robots can think like humans. (True/False)
6. Excel is a tool used mainly for drawing pictures. (True/False)
7. A CPU is a type of software. (True/False)
8. You need an email account to send and receive emails. (True/False)
9. Coding is only used in games. (True/False)
10. A search engine is used to browse the internet. (True/False)

One Word – **(1 X 10 = 10 marks)**

1. What is the main component of a computer that processes instructions?
2. Name one example of application software.
3. What device is used to print documents from a computer?
4. What is a collection of instructions in programming called?
5. Which device is used to type information into a computer?
6. What is the process of putting data into a computer called?
7. Name the tool used in Excel to perform calculations.
8. What do we call the collection of pages on the Internet?

9. Which software is used to create digital presentations?
10. What system allows computers to connect and share information worldwide?

Choose the Correct Option – **(1 X 10 = 10 marks)**

1. What is the full form of CPU?
A) Central Program Unit
B) Central Processing Unit
C) Computer Processing Unit
D) Core Processing Unit

2. Which of these is an output device?
A) Keyboard
B) Mouse
C) Monitor
D) Scanner

3. What is the primary function of an operating system?
A) To play music
B) To manage computer resources
C) To create drawings
D) To browse the internet

4. Which software is used for creating spreadsheets?
A) Word
B) Excel
C) Paint
D) PowerPoint

5. What does an algorithm do?
A) Stores data
B) Solves problems step-by-step
C) Connects devices
D) Displays graphics

6. Which key combination is used to copy text?
A) Ctrl + A
B) Ctrl + C
C) Ctrl + V
D) Ctrl + X

7. Which of these is an example of an application software?
A) Windows
B) Excel
C) CPU
D) Keyboard

8. In Excel, rows are labeled by:
A) Numbers

B) Letters
C) Symbols
D) Shapes

9. Which device helps us to connect to the Internet?
A) CPU
B) Printer
C) Modem
D) Keyboard

10. Which of these is a search engine?
A) Windows
B) Google
C) Word
D) Excel

SECTION-B

Short Question- **(2 X 5 = 10 marks)**

1. Explain the role of the CPU in a computer.
2. Describe the difference between hardware and software. Give one example of each.
3. Why is it important to stay safe online? Mention two ways to stay safe.
4. What is the purpose of PowerPoint, and how is it useful?
5. Briefly explain what coding is and why it is important.

ADDITIONAL RESOURCE

NEP
Link: https://youtu.be/6sKTXOY_yFw
QR Code:

Credit Score:
Link: https://youtu.be/NxMHHIt9PcI
QR Code:

CBSE:
Link: https://youtu.be/uOkCDapmhKc
QR Code: